THE NEXT ELVIS

BARBARA BARNES SIMS

THE NEXT ELVIS

SEARCHING FOR STARDOM AT SUN RECORDS

LOUISIANA STATE UNIVERSITY PRESS | BATON ROUGE

Published by Louisiana State University Press

lsupress.org

LOUISIANA PAPERBACK EDITION, 2024

DESIGNER: *Mandy McDonald Scallan*

TYPEFACE: *Whitman*

This book is a personal recollection. All names, dates, and events herein are accurate
to the best of the author's knowledge, and all opinions expressed are hers.

Library of Congress Cataloging-in-Publication Data

Sims, Barbara Barnes, 1933–

  The next Elvis : searching for stardom at Sun Records / Barbara Barnes Sims.

    pages cm

  Includes index.

  ISBN 978-0-8071-5798-5 (cloth : alk. paper) — ISBN 978-0-8071-5799-2 (pdf) — ISBN
978-0-8071-5800-5 (epub) — ISBN 978-0-8071-8173-7 (paperback) 1. Sims, Barbara
Barnes, 1933– 2. Sound recording industry—Tennessee—Memphis—Employees—Bi-
ography. 3. Sun Records—History. 4. Phillips, Sam, 1923–2003. I. Title.

  ML429.S57A3 2014

  781.64092—dc23

  [B]

2014006075

In memory of family members—Robert, Susie, Maude, and Eleanor—whose love and encouragement continue to sustain me,

For my daughter Sue,

And for Will, who inspired me to tell this story.

If the origin of a music can be traced to any one source, for rock 'n' roll that source would be Sun. And if there is one man without whom the revolution which took place in American popular music seems difficult to imagine, that man is Sam Phillips.

—PETER GURALNICK, *Feel Like Going Home* (E. P. Dutton, 1971)

. . . four women employees, Phillips says, run the business.

—EDWIN HOWARD, quoting Sam Phillips, "He's Made $2 Million on Disks—Without a Desk," *Memphis Press-Scimitar*, April 29, 1959

CONTENTS

Illustrations follow pages 84 and 141.

PREFACE

Lightning doesn't strike twice in the same place—everybody knows that. But still they came. The procession of singers and guitar pickers to 706 Union Avenue, Memphis, began after Elvis Presley crazed the nation's teenagers as he exploded on the music scene in 1954. A constant stream of hopefuls crossed the threshold of the unassuming Memphis Recording Service, home of Sun Records, each convinced he could be the Next Elvis. All he needed was for Sam Phillips to hear him—that would be the crucial break.

I was witness to this phenomenon during the brief, exciting time of the early days of rock 'n' roll. Even though I came to Sun after Elvis had moved on to RCA and eventually the Army, my time with the company was a unique education. Working with Sam Phillips and Sun in sales, publicity, and promotion, I absorbed much from Sam's remarkable mind and unique personality, at the same time witnessing the development of some of his great discoveries—the triumphs and the disasters. Just as memorable to me were the little day-to-day happenings that have kept the Sun years alive in my mind. Some of these incidents portray how the music industry worked as I observed it from 1957 to 1960, during Sun's ascendancy and later as the major labels were again consolidating their power. Just as Sam Phillips's ability to see potential in the raw talent of Elvis and many who followed him, it also afforded opportunities for women in roles usually not open to them in the 1950s. That is how I came to be one of the seven employees who, with Sam, comprised the Sun staff in its glory years.

I have always been grateful to Sam for having faith in me and giving me the opportunity to be a part of his story. Late in his life, he said that when people tell of him, his only wish was that they would tell the truth. I have tried to be truthful about him and all the other people who appear on these pages. When I quote conversations, they are mostly ones I can recall almost verbatim, but in some places, where stereotyped situations like answering the phone or being introduced to someone are presented, I have put words in some mouths. The passage of many years has dulled my memory of certain details, but the anecdotes I recount are essentially vivid recall. I was aided by written records concerning the chronology of sessions, release dates of records, the weather on a certain day, and other facts of this nature.

Though Elvis was no longer at Sun when I arrived, his presence and his story remained a part of the scene at Sun; hence the title. The whole Sun story is predicated on the fact that Sam Phillips from his early years knew and loved the musical language and the evocative power of black music. In its beginning Sun recorded many outstanding blues musicians. Sam was pleased with the music he was producing with his black artists, but he wanted greater commercial success. His experience had told him that, because of the racist attitudes expressed in the segregation of music as in society as a whole, a black blues or R&B artist in the United States in the 1950s couldn't hope to enjoy the commercial success of a Frank Sinatra in the pop field or a Marty Robbins in the country field. He told his associates that if he could find the right young white singer, he could make both of them rich.

Music fans know the story of how Phillips groomed, recorded, and promoted Presley until he gained commercial viability, only to sell him to RCA Victor (and allied management and music-publishing interests) for a sum that seems paltry by today's standards. But Sam never looked back, instead insisting that the sale of Elvis gave his firm greater financial strength and thus the ability to look for the Next Elvis. He didn't use those words, but discovering exceptional talent was his goal, and in the succeeding years he helped launch some outstanding musical careers.

The First, the Real, the Only Elvis was a real-live walking, talking, shaking, singing phenomenon born in the imagination of a record producer who, like his studio, seemed fairly ordinary until one got into his mind. It was as if he had willed Elvis to come to him. He didn't know that the person he was seeking would have sideburns or rubber legs or a screwy name, but he knew he had to find a sexy young white man who could sing with the kind of gritty abandon that black southern blues performers were known for.

Some of the others who followed Elvis at Sun during my years with the company were memorable as well. Carl Perkins, Roy Orbison, Jerry Lee Lewis, and Charlie Rich were among those who came after Elvis and carved for themselves a lasting niche in American music. Many of lesser talent or not as much luck came and struck out. Several recorded briefly at Sun and then went on to gain success elsewhere. Of course, no one became the Next Elvis, because there is only one King. In the meantime, my own personal and professional development was proceeding, as I left my sheltered upbringing for a larger, more exciting world.

I hope you enjoy reading of how the search for stardom went on, amidst the joys and frustrations of the days at Sun after Elvis.

THE NEXT ELVIS

ONE

——— ☆ ———

1957

Whole Lot of Shakin' Going On

JERRY LEE LEWIS (SUN 267)*

I Meet the Man Who Discovered Elvis Presley

Sam Phillips discovered Elvis, Johnny Cash, Carl Perkins, Jerry Lee Lewis, Roy Orbison, and some lesser-known rock and country musicians. Leo Soroka discovered me, or so the girls at Sam's company would say to tease me. Leo recommended me to Sam for a promotion and publicity job at Sun Record Company.

Like so many young women from small towns throughout the mid-South, I had come to Memphis looking for work. I aspired to use my college training in radio-TV and journalism, so in late 1956 I applied for a reporting job at United Press. The bureau head, Leo Soroka, wanted to hire me for the evening desk, a job that would include covering night court. Leo's bosses were astonished that he would even consider sending a young woman out on the Memphis streets at night. Result, no job, and instead I settled for tamer work in the sales promotion department of WMCT Television. Months later, when Sam ran into Leo at the Variety

---

*Sun catalog numbers were stamped on each disk. Later releases gave the title of the Jerry Lee hit as "Whole Lotta Shakin'," but the label of the original release read "Whole Lot of Shakin' Going On."

Club and mentioned he was searching for a woman with a journalism background, Leo told him about me. Sam rang me up the next day. That was in the summer of 1957.

We made an appointment to meet downtown for lunch at noon, but about eleven o'clock, Sam's assistant, Sally Wilbourn, called to say he couldn't make it. We rescheduled at least twice, but each time he cancelled at the last minute. Then, one evening about eight o'clock, Sam called and, saying he was sorry none of our appointments had worked out, told me he was free right then and wondered if it would be OK if he came right over to my apartment to talk. I lived in "the medical center" neighborhood not too far from Sun's studios, so in fifteen minutes he was there, all five-feet-ten-inches of him. He was wearing white ducks, a white shirt, and a sailor cap. He had a thatch of brown wavy hair with golden streaks, a dark tan, and an almost tangible energy that somehow seemed to be transmitted in his handshake. He walked right in like we were old friends, flashing a very wide and sort of confidential smile. There was the slightest bit of a crocodile grin to those curling lips and gleaming teeth. He was completely at ease, not to say instantly in control of the situation.

He surveyed my apartment in a glance and then fixed me with his piercing blue eyes. They had an intensity I had seen only in Billy Graham in his TV close-ups. The two were alike, I thought, as Sam started talking nonstop in a way that reminded me of preaching. He was telling me about his company, Sun Records, and all the many tasks running the company involved, and how I could help him with these duties. He talked fast, with dramatic pauses and stinging emphasis on certain words. He was overflowing with enthusiasm, but the ideas were tumbling out so fast that I couldn't quite follow all the information—hit records, TV shows, artists, LPs, singles, pressing plants, names I'd never heard, too much at once.

I managed to blurt out, "Excuse me, but I have to take care of something. My water heater has sprung a leak." Embarrassed by this inopportune development that I had noticed just about the time he had called, I got up and emptied the pan under the tank. After that, he very matter-of-factly began to take turns emptying the water as it accumulated, so unceremoniously that our conversation was uninterrupted. I decided he was tactful, efficient, and in a way humble.

Sam didn't ask for a résumé or even want to talk about my qualifications. He seemed to know me already. Perhaps Leo had told him a few facts about my work background. When I asked Sam exactly what I would be doing for him, he spread his arms out wide and exclaimed, "Barbara, you are going to be doing so many things. From one day to the next, you will be surprised at just what you will be doing. Talking to these distributors and disk jockeys, writing about these artists, hyping *Billboard* and *Cashbox*—every day there's going to be something different. You are going to love it—don't get me wrong, I am devoted to radio, but it's nothing like this record business." The reference to radio pertained to his career in radio that had begun when he was a teenager in Alabama and continued into the time he founded Sun.

Getting Down to Business

When I asked for more specifics, he said the first thing he needed was some liner notes for the backs of his first two album releases. He pulled out an acetate of Carl Perkins songs and put it on my record player. When I said I knew "Blue Suede Shoes" and had danced to it, he grabbed my hand and we stood up and started to bop in my tiny carpeted living room. He had on white bucks, and he moved his small feet in a close-together shuffle. He held his head to one side while dancing. You could tell he really liked Carl Perkins' rhythm, which I did, too. Very much. I told him I thought I could write liner notes for this album.

In a minute or two, we sat down and he started to play Johnny Cash's album. Sam studied my reaction and intuited that I wasn't instantly taken with the music. He said, "I believe you like Carl better." True, I did. With Perkins, I was in familiar territory, but Cash's dark country sound was new and different to me, haunting and hard to absorb. I hadn't been conscious of Cash, even though he had had a couple of successful records by then. But I agreed to keep this array of songs too and see what I could write.

That satisfied Sam, and we didn't talk about full-time work. Instead,

I told him I'd do the liner notes on a freelance basis and call him as soon as I had something. Then he left me to ponder this odd job interview, this unusual person, and this fascinating new music that, had I known it, would make the Sun label recognizable the world over.

A New Kind of Writing Assignment

Later that evening, I listened to those acetates again, and when I woke up the next morning, I put them on another time. As I dressed for work, I listened intently as the needle moved slowly over the grooves, first Cash and then Perkins. At work during the day, every now and then the thump-thump of the bass on Johnny's record or the ringing tones of the guitar introduction to "Blue Suede Shoes" would flit through my mind.

After my day at WMCT, it was a relief to get off that hot bus that brought me from downtown Memphis to my nice air-conditioned apartment. It felt good to shed the belted shirtwaist and clingy nylon slip I'd been wearing and sit on the sofa, staring straight ahead at the skinny martini pitcher on top of my tea cart—two of my first purchases for my little home. A green pitcher from my grandaddy's farm in Mississippi held some daisies. I looked but hardly saw them as I pondered what I might say about the music I was supposed to introduce to prospective record buyers.

I had been earning money from writing for a long time. I got a start at the *Daily Corinthian* in my hometown of Corinth, Mississippi, while in high school. Then I worked at the University of Alabama news bureau and the educational TV station, and now nearly three years out of college, I had had full-time writing experience, with an ad agency and two TV stations. I had written commercials about everything from Morning Treat Coffee to industrial engines, but never anything having to do with music. Somehow this assignment seemed more important than ordinary ad copy. I hoped I could tune in to what these singers were trying to convey and how they were doing it.

Finally, I took my Royal portable from its speckled gray case and placed it on the dinette table. I would tackle Carl Perkins and his band first, and this copy came pretty easily. As Sam had observed, I just naturally responded to his infectious music. Carl's beat, his sound, was pretty close to the rhythm and blues that I had heard and enjoyed. I had heard it on WLAC, Nashville, also on a station from an African American college in Fort Valley, Georgia, during my first year of college in Macon, and from those crazy DJs on New Orleans radio when I worked there for some months.

I opened my notes by saying the album might be called *Carl Perkins Sings Carl Perkins* because only two of the tracks on the album came from other songwriters. There never would have been an album, of course, except for "Blue Suede Shoes," which had made music history by being the first record ever to score big on all three *Billboard* charts—pop, country, and R&B.

It was the R&B placement that was extraordinary, in that pop and especially country-sounding artists hadn't before achieved that success, and Carl's record climbed to #2. For pop, he also arrived at #2, for part of the time topped only by an Elvis smash. "Blue Suede Shoes" became Sun's first million-seller.

Sam had the cover designed and named it *Carl Perkins Dance Album*, referring, as I noted, to the exuberance of the music that made people want to get up and dance—"feel good music," as Carl called it. Carl's guitar solos were playful, exceptionally fresh and fun, contributing greatly to the overall effect.

In the notes, I stated that Carl was from Jackson, Tennessee, and at age twenty-three was the father of three children. Maybe not a good profile for a rising rock star, but I didn't think of that. The tunes I liked most on the album were "Matchbox," which he adapted from an old blues tune, and ones he had penned, "Your True Love" and "Honey Don't."

I chose not to mention "Sure to Fall" and some of the other cuts that had a strong hillbilly flavor, because I liked them least. The sentimentality that I found in some country music didn't appeal to me, and this attitude proved a stumbling block I couldn't avoid as I tried to shape a response to the Johnny Cash album. Cash's music struck me as complex—primitive in a way, yet too penetrating to peg as just another country act. Besides, there were no fiddles.

As I listened to Cash, I came to like the music more and more and was able to pick out three themes that seemed to run through all the material. What I heard Johnny Cash expressing were qualities of loneliness, romantic longing, and religious fervor, and I wrote about the tunes that exemplified each of these. For example, the album included "So Dog-gone Lonesome" and "I Heard that Lonesome Whistle Blow," which were perfect for what I called his "rangy, big, hollow voice." Melancholy wasn't his only mood, as shown by the joyful "I Was There When It Happened," a religious song. For love, there were "Cry, Cry, Cry" and "I Walk the Line," one of his big hits. I could have added a fourth category, prisons, and featured "Folsom Prison Blues" (six weeks on the country chart and a pop crossover as well) and "Doin' My Time," but I chose to leave it with the magic number of three.

Instead, I fleshed out the notes with references to his childhood hard-ships in Arkansas, his time in military service, which he termed "three long, miserable years" in Germany, and the launching of his Sun record-ing career. In 1956, he had been named "the most promising country and western artist of the year" in four major national music polls.

There was more to say about Johnny, his talents as a songwriter (I couldn't fit into the allotted space my favorite, "Big River"), his diverse musical roots, his band, the Tennessee Two. To me he seemed the em-bodiment of a contemporary folk singer, and that's the aspect of his music that touched me most. I ended the notes with this observation: "To hear this Johnny Cash album is to know Johnny Cash—the man, the lonely dreamer with a stubborn streak of realism that makes for strong and unforgettable conversation in song." Sam subsequently named the album *Johnny Cash with His Hot and Blue Guitar*. Once the notes were done, I made a clean copy of each piece, with a carbon to keep, and settled down with a cold Budweiser to listen to the jazz DJ on WREC.

So This Is Where They Make the Records

The next day I couldn't wait to deliver the finished copy into the hands of Sam Phillips, but when I dropped by after work, he wasn't in. I was so informed by the woman I'd been talking with on the phone, Sam's secretary, Sally Wilbourn. She was a petite, brown-haired, very fresh and slightly freckled young woman, who promised to give the pages I'd written to Sam. Another young woman was sitting at a desk, glancing my way briefly while talking with a tall man standing by the door who gave me a frank appraisal. About the time I came in, a couple of guys followed me and walked through the office without speaking to anyone. Sally said, "Y'all, this is Barbara Barnes. Sam is getting her to do some publicity work for us." Then she introduced Sun's receptionist, Regina Reese, and the man, whom she identified as Sam's brother, Jud. They nodded and resumed talking with each other.

The Sun offices and studio were located almost at the corner where Manassas dead-ended into Union, about three blocks west of Beale. The address was 706 Union Avenue, on "automobile row," an area where used and new car dealers and auto parts stores lined the street. Sun's office was quite small and seemed crowded with the three people in there working among the two desks, two file cabinets (one tall and one short), and a couple of phones. A Naugahyde-covered loveseat sat in front of a big glass window that had a closed blind. Linoleum tiles covered the floor, and the glass entrance door had a saggy venetian blind to shut out the afternoon sun. A blue neon sign on the window read, "Memphis Recording Service." By appearances, this outfit wasn't that big a deal, and I wondered if they were making any money. I left disappointed that I hadn't seen Sam and about the shabbiness of my prospective place of employment.

I shared my opinion when I phoned Leo Soroka to report on my first visit to Sun. He replied in his Brooklyn speak, "Ya know what they call it, don't ya?"

"No, what?"

"It's a hole in the wall completely surrounded by Cadillacs."

Sun's Sister Company Is Born—Phillips International

Sure enough, I saw a white Cadillac convertible parked at the curb when I next visited Sun. Sam had called to say the liner notes were "fine—just fine, you said it just right, like I wanted it" and asked me to come in again to talk about further work. A friend from WMCT was dropping me off at the studio at just the same time a man was parking his motorcycle near the front door. I said, "That's Sam Phillips's brother, Jud. He's the sales manager of the company." We laughed to imagine what it would take to get a manager from stuffy old WMCT on a motorcycle.

Jud grinned upon seeing me and gallantly opened the door. He had a smooth manner and deep Alabama accent, asking as we stepped into the office how I was bearing up under the heat. Sally, looking up from her desk to say "hi," was surrounded by a crush of young men sitting on the love seat or standing near the studio door. Jud's six feet contributed to the crowding. Sam was standing with one foot propped on Regina's desk, talking on the phone. He motioned he'd be right with me and, when he hung up, he said, "Let's get out of here," suggesting we have a bite downtown. He had said he wanted to get me to write a brochure to introduce a new company he was launching, Sam C. Phillips International.

On the way out, he said, "That's the only way I can get some quiet. I do most of my business from home or in a café," he explained. "Somebody is always coming in or else the phone is ringing, somebody wanting to talk to me." I had noticed there didn't seem to be enough room for him, either. "Jud, we'll get together later," he called back over his shoulder.

We walked out into the heat and that Memphis humidity that always made me feel like I was carrying a box on my head. The curl in my hair had long since begun to droop. I assumed he wanted to go to the café next door, but he motioned to his white Cadillac with those sleek fins. It was the first one I'd ever ridden in, and I sort of wished we could have the top down, though the air conditioning felt good. He pulled up into an empty space in front of Dinstuhl's candy shop, and we got out to be assailed again by the heat. The sun was beginning its arc over the Mississippi River Bridge and would soon descend right into the flat cotton fields of West Memphis. Downtown Memphis had emptied out its office workers, and a ghostly feeling was taking over as people had deserted the streets for the suburbs.

We jaywalked over to Anderton's restaurant, one of Memphis's few seafood places. Anderton's had a lobster tank, red Naugahyde seats in the booths, dusty fake foliage, and an extensive menu. As soon as we ordered, Sam began to talk. He said that, in launching his new label, he wanted a brochure he could send to wholesale distributors, the trade papers, Sun's foreign associates, music publishers, and others in the industry. He wanted to explain his vision for the label and introduce himself, his staff, and some of the musicians he was going to release on Phillips International.

The publication would be designed by an artist, Andy Anderson, whose studio was next door to the restaurant in the Goodwyn Institute Building. It happened to be where I worked in the WMCT studios. Sam showed me the logo Andy had already designed for the new company, a blue-and-green globe on a white background, which would be used for stationery. The label on the 45s would have a pale blue background (suggesting oceans) with darker blue continents. The Phillips name would have the two "l's" connected like musical sixteenth notes, and the printing for the name of the song and the artist would be red. A red-and-white ribbon faintly suggesting the American flag waving under the Phillips name read "International Corp." It was sort of a literal and corny design, I thought, but the stationery was crisp and heavy. I had seen the Sun stationery and thought it was a little funky, orange with burnt-umber printing on flimsy paper.

Sam Tells Me His Life Story

Sam was easy to talk with. We had some common ground as natives of small towns in the Tennessee Valley who had pursued careers in broadcasting, though it was obvious he was much further along in life than I was, and not just the ten years in age. I soon learned he not only had a recording company but also a wife and two sons, a ranch house with pool, a Cadillac, a radio station, and maybe more for all I knew. At one point, I provided an opening for the story of how he got into the record business, as I remarked that the Muzak in the background was playing a song I liked. I had no idea that my remark would set Sam off. Sam exclaimed, "I've been away from that kind of music so long that I don't even know what that song is." He added vehemently, "That kind of music is what made me get into the business of making records."

"I was doing remotes every night from the Peabody Hotel." Here he assumed a very melodious and pompous radio-announcer voice and intoned: "Good evening, ladies and gentlemen. We are broadcasting from the romantic Skyway, high atop Hotel Peabody, overlooking Ol' Man River, here in Memphis, Tennessee." For these broadcasts, he was the engineer, not the announcer, but he did have an expressive, even memorable, speaking voice. I guessed it was partly natural endowment and part on-the-job polishing.

"So you were an announcer?" I asked. He admitted he'd had that role on stations in Florence, Alabama, as well as Nashville and Memphis, but added, "I never was anything like the greatest announcer." I liked this further sign of his humility, because all the announcers I'd known worshipped their own voices.

"Man, every night it was the same old stuff," he continued, quite animated. "Every band that came through played the same tunes in the same tired old way. It was so stereotyped. There was no life to it. I knew there had to be other people that felt the same way I did—ready to hear something different! Something new!"

I understood and knew he was right. My friend who was working his way through Memphis State as a security officer in the Skyway made fun of the music, saying, "All it's good for is for those squares to do their businessman's bounce." Music publishers put out arrangements of dance music that were used by bands large and small throughout the country. We used them in the high-school band I played piano with, and I heard them at college dances.

Sam Gets Started in the Recording Business

Sam found an escape from WREC and the boring bands in his talent for sound engineering. "I talked to my wife and told her I wanted to take a gamble on a recording studio. My goal was to find some performers throughout the mid-South and make the kind of records the black people, and some young white people, were buying. I knew there was a lot of talent in the Memphis area that wasn't being heard.

"To keep the doors open, I also operated a recording service. This started in 1950. We would go out and record funerals, weddings, or any kind of event the people wanted to keep on record. Also, people could come in and make a personal recording. Some of them wanted to see how they sounded, and others wanted to record a message to send off to loved ones. Some had dreams of becoming recording artists. Our motto was 'We Record Anything, Anywhere, Anytime.'" He gave a grin, but I couldn't tell if it was sheepish or prideful.

Sam got really wound up telling me how he felt and what he thought in getting his studio going—the wealth of talent from the Mississippi and Arkansas deltas to be heard on Beale Street, the electronic advances in recording, the expanding market for recordings, and other favorable conditions at that time.

At first he recorded black artists, some of whom were, as he had been, radio announcers. These, though, were all on black radio stations, chiefly WDIA in Memphis. "Blues Boy" King, later known as B.B. King, was one of them. Little Junior Parker and Howlin' Wolf came along and gave Sam some commercial success in selling these sides to independent record labels—Chess and Checker in Chicago and Modern on the West Coast.

An hour had passed and Sam was still going strong, as he explained that this system broke down and he was almost forced to manufacture and sell his records for himself. He seemed to be reliving a traumatic period, describing how he had to beg distributors to market his records and radio stations to play them. Traveling to small towns, sleeping in YMCAs, existing on coffee and lunchmeat sandwiches, he held on to the dream of making a success of his company, which he christened "Sun Records."

"With all that traveling everywhere from Alabama to Texas, we managed to make some regional charts in Memphis, Nashville, and New Orleans, plus we also got some unexpected breaks with Presley," Sam said. "Listeners in some cities, including Detroit and Los Angeles, liked his music, blacks and whites alike. They'd been listening to lots of R&B. Bill Randle in Cleveland took to Elvis. He liked jazz and blues, so he found something in Presley he could relate to. He had a big following."

Because the Memphis papers reported every move Elvis made, Sam assumed I knew all about him and how Sam had sold his contract for $40,000. "This gave me the capital to really get into business. Up to then, I never knew if I was going to be able to pay the rent the next month. I got hit with a big excise tax bill I didn't even know I owed. Then Don Robey out in Houston sued me about 'Bear Cat.' Said our artist, Rufus Thomas, lifted most of it from one of his releases.

"Selling Elvis made it possible for me to invest in Carl and Johnny and to put Jud out on the road with them. Now we have Jerry Lee, and this man is going to be big! He's a native! No one anywhere has ever recorded an artist like Jerry Lee Lewis! Not only can he play and sing, he is a fantastic showman!" At this point, Sam was practically jumping out of his seat, leaning toward me, drawing out the syllables of his words, as in fann-tasss-tic. His eyes were blazing with conviction, like an evangelist preaching the gospel.

"I need to go home pretty soon," I finally managed to insert, and he picked up on it. We left, and he dropped me at home very politely.

"Call me if you have any questions," he said. "You can call me at home. Do you have that number?"

I said, "I'll get it from Sally if I need it. I think I have enough. Thank you for the dinner." He drove away, and I had another project to sort out in my mind. I smiled to myself as a quote from Shakespeare came to mind: "O brave new world, that hath such people in it."

Back to the Promotion Piece

I had some sketchy notes, but I wondered about Phillips International. Sam said that he wanted to go in a different, more musically diverse, direction with Phillips International, but he didn't say why he needed another label to do this. I knew it was common for recording companies, actually all kinds of businesses, to have subsidiaries, maybe having to do with taxes. He said he would keep the distributors who were doing well with Sun, but try out others with Phillips International where the distributor wasn't selling much.

The staff and some of the artists he planned to feature on PI had been with Sun, but others would be introduced for the first time. I was eager to talk with Jud, with engineer-producer Jack Clement, and with the musical director, Bill Justis, who, Sam said, was going to have an instrumental release to launch the label. Maybe I'd get to meet some of the singers, too. Later, when I wrote the brochure, I didn't mention the questions in my mind about the need for a new label, I just wrote what Sam had told me were his goals: "(1) to develop new talent and (2) to bring universal acceptance to the country and race music which a majority of people either shunned or furtively enjoyed when there was no one around to take note."

Those weren't his words—his discussion was much more colorful and animated as he reminded me of what I already knew, that middle-class America respected only classical or pop music and considered other genres contaminated with their lower-class associations. Hillbillies and bluesmen did not belong in polite society.

I was able to do some short interviews in preparation for writing the brochure. Jack Clement brought a heavily made-up and buxom singer, Barbara Pittman, to meet me at the Peabody Hotel coffee shop during my lunch hour one day. Bill Justis, who was on tour, spoke to me by phone, and Hayden Thompson met me at the studio. He was the only one who had the pompadour and sulky good looks of a possible Elvis successor. The fourth new talent featured in the brochure was a country singer, Buddy Blake, who appeared by his photo to have passed the time he could be a contender for stardom among record-buying teens. Regina had a sheet made up on him that I used to write his blurb.

Sam Phillips himself was the subject of much of the brochure's content. I said I liked him, but I tweaked his self-confidence (not to say ego), writing that he was his own best press-agent and that "I believe in Sam, almost as much as Sam believes in Sam." Also, I noted his interest in the religious and spiritual realms and his early ambition to be a minister. It was a bit of a puff piece, reporting him to be "honest, straightforward, even-tempered, congenial," and tenacious, but I expressed doubts of his description of himself as "the simplest man you ever met." To me he seemed to possess a very complicated and calculating mind. As time wore on and I came to know Sam better, I would be able to judge whether my first impressions of him were correct and whether what he told me of himself was always accurate.

I got the copy together and dropped it off at the studio, where Regina assembled the necessary pictures and sent the piece to the graphic designer, Andy. Later that week, I rode up the elevator from my office to his to read the proofs when he had the layout ready to go to the printer. Shortly afterwards, I dropped by the Sun studio to get some copies of the finished product. Sally informed me, "The boxes came yesterday, and the brochures are already being mailed out."

Another Sun VIP

At that time, I met another important member of Sam's team, his lawyer, Roy Scott. He was well dressed, neat, of medium height and build, balding, with a somewhat morose long face, except when he smiled, and then he looked kind of sly.

"We were going over to the Toddle House, Barbara. You want to come along?"

"Fine with me," I said, and we loaded up in Sam's Cadillac, but Roy wanted to drive his cute little green MG so he could go home after his conversation with Sam.

Perched on three adjacent stools, we carried on a conversation while Roy and I had hamburgers and Sam had eggs and bacon. He explained, "This is morning to me. Sometimes I get to bed late and sleep until afternoon. I'm like a baby that's got his days and nights mixed up." He added that he became a night person when he worked the Peabody remotes at night and afterwards often recorded into the wee hours.

I felt somewhat unnecessary as Roy launched into the business matters that had brought him to the studio that evening. Some of the talk concerned radio station WHER, which was one of Sam's enterprises. When I asked about the station, they explained that the studio was in the first Holiday Inn location and that the founder of the new motel chain, Kemmons Wilson, was a partner of Sam's. Roy was a lawyer for Holiday Inn as well as for Sun, and he and Sam both had stock in Holiday Inn.

Then they took off on another subject which I couldn't follow, but Sam was getting heated about some business matters. I heard unfamiliar names, the words "contract," "distributor," and so on. At one point Sam turned to me and said, "One thing you have to get ready for in this business. Not everybody plays by the rules. There are some unscrupulous characters that are always looking for a sucker. Somebody they can bleed."

I said, "What you're saying is that they expect everybody to screw them, so they decide, 'I'll screw you first.'"

Sam exclaimed, "That's exactly right! You get my meaning, and I like the way you phrased it."

Southern ladies just didn't talk that way in the '50s, but I had picked up a few new words since I began working in radio and newspapering. I hadn't been trying to impress Sam Phillips, but I was happy my remark did.

Roy said goodnight after a while, and Sam and I took off in the Cadillac with the top down. The breeze felt good though the air was still very hot. Sam mentioned the brochure again, saying he was surprised when he read what I'd written. "I said to myself, 'This woman knows me.'" He repeated it with great emphasis.

"Well, don't other people know you?" He didn't give me a direct answer, so I pursued it further, saying, "Who do you confide in?"

He asserted, almost defiantly, "I don't confide in anyone." Period.

Then we drove up to the curb by my building, and he let me out. Again, I had something to think about concerning Sam. What had led him to be closed off that way? He had seemed so accessible.

What Does This Mean?

A couple of hours after Sam left me at home, the phone rang and it was Sally Wilbourn. She sounded like she had been crying.

"Barbara, when you and Sam left, did he ask me to go along with you and Roy?" she asked.

"Gosh, Sally. I can't remember. There was a lot going on."

"He says he did, but he did not. If he would have asked me, I would have gone," she continued.

"Well, Sally, I don't think it's important. We didn't talk about much. Just had a hamburger. It was mostly Sam and Roy talking about business."

"Yes, but he said he did, and I know he didn't ask me!"

"I tell you what. I think you need to go to sleep and forget about it. Do you have any Equanil or Miltown? Take one of those and go to sleep. It's not worth worrying about."

She had wanted a "yes" or "no," but either would have been the wrong answer. I sensed I was getting into waters I hadn't suspected might exist.

A Surprising Memory

Sally's call left me feeling unsettled. At bedtime, I lay awake staring at the ceiling, playing WREC very low and thinking about what tomorrow at WMCT would hold. That job was a disappointment. I was supposed to work in sales service, but somehow the salesmen never had enough work for me to do. I'd been lucky to get the job, which was a notch above the clerical work that women were usually confined to. My degree in radio-TV prepared me for more than I was doing, though.

Then I went over what I'd heard Sam and Roy talking about and what they had said about WHER. Then it popped into my head! I'd been there! When I came to Memphis looking for work in January, I had gone way out on Summer Avenue to meet a woman named Dotty Abbott. She was assistant manager of WHER radio, and she described the owner as a "very attractive and dynamic" young man who had launched this station, the first ever to be entirely staffed by women. They ran the board, sold the ads, read the news, and played the records—they did everything except engineer the tower. I had applied for a job in sales, and she thought I'd be good. She had set up a meeting with her boss at a restaurant.

The memories came together with a jolt. Of course!! The man I went to see was Sam Phillips! How could I have forgotten! Why hadn't he remembered me? I had certainly liked him. Suddenly I could vividly recall sitting there in a booth—I was facing the door—with Sam. That day he was wearing a coat and tie and seemed much older and more serious than the jaunty, insouciant fellow who had turned up at my door. He had said very little, instead just listening to me talk about myself. At that time, I had vaguely heard of Elvis and Sun, but the name Sam Phillips was not familiar to me. So I didn't connect him with the record business, but only WHER. I was preoccupied that day, too, knowing that I was due later at an employment agency in the Sterick Building and then at WMCT TV. My mother was waiting to drive me to the next interview and then back home to Corinth that night.

Still, once I made the connection, I could recall how we were drinking coffee and he was asking me about my experience and why I wanted to be in sales. I had told him frankly that I was tired of being a copywriter and I didn't want to be on the air, but that I thought I could be good at sales. My professors had told me there was money to be made in sales, so that part interested me quite a bit.

I told him about my work before, during, and after college, all having to do with radio, TV, journalism, or advertising. He listened intently, as if he were totally concentrating on and thinking about what I was saying, nodding and not interrupting until I had finished my spiel. I recall thinking how nice it was to be taken seriously. He asked a question or two, with a penetrating gaze. You could almost see the wheels turning in his mind.

Then our talks reached a dead end. I had to tell him I didn't have a car. He seemed genuinely sorry and sympathetic to learn about my situation. But, he said, "A car is one essential for selling time in Memphis. This town is so spread out, you couldn't get around otherwise." I was crestfallen. That is how I came to accept the offer I received later that day from WMCT.

Now I was on the brink of working for Sam Phillips again, and this time, I mused, it might really happen. One little thing nagged at the back of my mind. At one of our meetings, Sam had said, "I want you to know my bad side." I didn't ask him to explain, and I guess I liked him so much and was so impressed that I dismissed the notion that he had a "bad side." Now I was wondering what he meant by that and thinking, "It surely can't be anything too bad. If I go to Sun Records, I'll find out in time, I guess." My thoughts trailed off, and sleep finally came.

Another Phillips Phenomenon

It wasn't long after I finished working on the Phillips International brochure that Sam's attention turned to ways I could help with some Jerry Lee Lewis promotion. One evening, he brought Jud over to the apartment to help persuade me to go to work full-time. Jud's promotion talents were key in building Jerry Lee Lewis's career and keeping him on the top in the rock 'n' roll world. Before this night, no more than a casual "hello" had passed between us, so I welcomed the chance to get to know Jud and find out more about this whole Sun setup. Sam pointed out that, even though Jud was on the road more than in the office, we would work closely together if I came to work for Sun. He would need me to feed him information about orders and issues with distributors, as well as keep up with radio station personnel and anything else pertaining to sales and promotion.

Seen side by side, the two brothers were entirely different, I could see that right away. Sam was all energy, quick and vigorous, compact, with powerful rays shooting out from him. This force at times made him seem a little dangerous, not at all the cuddly type, though he could be very charming.

Jud was the older of the two. He was tall, thin, and just slightly stooped, with long bones in his arms, legs, and hands. His clothes hung on him the way designers want their clothes to hang on models. Later he told me that when he flew sometimes people on the airplane would ask if he were a movie star, and he did look as if he could have come out of a western. He had blue eyes, brown hair, and a face that was slightly acne-scarred, which made him even more interesting looking. He had a widow's peak on his forehead, just as Sam did, and a wide smile that was at once self-deprecating and a little mischievous. I thought he was very disarming—a bashful boy, a teddy bear you could hug and call "sweetie." He spoke with that deep Alabama drawl I had liked so much in other men I had met when I was at the university in Tuscaloosa.

Defending Rock 'n' Roll from the Philistines

On the evening Sam brought Jud over for the first time, they seemed to think, mistakenly, that maybe I was hesitating to work for them because I objected to rock 'n' roll on moral grounds. They went into a lengthy defense of rock 'n' roll, pointing out that Peggy Lee's current hit, "Fever," was as erotic as any Elvis Presley record. Personally, to me it seemed more so, because Elvis's wink and sly looks were ironic, even funny at times. Not so "Fever." After he'd pulled out his flask and proceeded to my little kitchen to make himself a drink, Jud pronounced, "People are pigs. You can wash them down, dress them up, make them look all fancy, sweet-smelling, and nice, but they're still pigs." Dirt made people like rock 'n' roll? He almost seemed to be agreeing with the preachers who condemned rock or J. Edgar Hoover, who had said that "rock is a corrupting influence." I didn't bother to disagree with Jud, but I didn't see anything evil about rock 'n' roll. What I heard at Sun seemed tame compared to those R&B hits like "Work with Me Annie" or "Sixty Minute Man." But it was hard to disagree with Jud when he got going. "A preacher just like his brother," I thought to myself. "Both missed their calling."

I ventured, "I have read that some of the preachers didn't like 'Blue Suede Shoes' because it refers to drinking. Lots of people think alcohol is a sign of sin and damnation." We agreed that since all of us had grown up Baptist in dry counties we knew this was true.

"But it's not just the Baptists," Jud disdainfully added. "That bishop of Chicago has banned R&B and rock 'n' roll from all Catholic campuses, so the kids have to dance to Perry Como and Guy Lombardo."

Finally we got to the part of the conversation about what Jud needed in his work with Jerry Lee. Sun was getting a ton of fan mail in reaction to "Whole Lot of Shakin' Going On" and they wanted me to start answering it. I said that the first thing I'd need was some stationery, and I asked for a picture of the new star to include in the design of the stationery I'd use to answer fan mail.

Sun Studio

I went by the next day to get it, and I was excited! It was a Saturday morning and I got to see the actual studio—not just the reception area—where Elvis, Johnny Cash, Carl Perkins, Roy Orbison, Jerry Lee, and all those blues singers had made their recordings. Jud walked me into the space, which was a long rectangle, saying, "Sam outfitted this studio himself. Look at the ceiling. The acoustic tile isn't flat the way you usually see it. He made curves in the ceiling with baffles to make the sound waves bounce the way he wanted them to. Sounds better that way."

It looked much like the studios in the radio stations I had worked in, except it had more stuff sitting around. A trash can was overflowing with beer cans and green wine bottles, and a folding metal chair held an ashtray full of cigarette butts. A guitar was sitting on a stand in one corner with a drum kit nearby. Several microphones were scattered around, and toward the control room there sat a small upright piano.

Warming up to the subject, Jud continued, "Sam is a genius in sound. My brother's got his ways, but there's nobody can touch him for sound. The trade papers are saying there's magic in 'the Sun sound.' He learned a lot from Mr. Wooten when we were at WREC. Now there's a man who knew sound."

"You were at WREC, too?" I asked.

"Not really. I just sang there in a gospel quartet. But I was the one who brought Sam here from Nashville." Sam had told me about his time there as an engineer and host of a record show, "Saturday Afternoon Tea Dance," which I had heard occasionally at home in Corinth at one time or another.

Then we were walking up the steps to the control room, and again things seemed familiar. The recording equipment looked like a radio station board, and a couple of reel-to-reel tape decks stood behind the chair facing the board. The back door of the control room led to a black emptiness that turned out to be a junk room when Jud switched on the light.

"These are returned records," he said, motioning to small square cardboard boxes scattered willy-nilly throughout the room. "Distributors have guarantees to return some of the stock they buy if it doesn't sell."

Then he opened a door to his right, and there I beheld a small office. "Sam has been thinking he needed an office, but what got him fired up is you coming to work. He had Jack Clement fix this up for you." I had asked Sam just where he intended to put me if I decided to accept his job offer, so here was his answer.

Jack was the engineer I had met a few weeks back, and according to

Jud he liked to build things. It was an easy task for him to erect the three needed walls. They had put in a window air conditioner, a file cabinet, a desk with a chair, and a swivel chair for a visitor. Jud looked into the file cabinet that had been installed there, along with a desk and chair. Under "artist photos" he pulled out a shot of Jerry Lee at the piano. "This ought to do, wouldn't it?" he said.

I agreed it would be fine and then promised to have Andy lay out the letterhead, which I would bring by as soon as possible. We were walking toward the front door, Jud saying, "You'll have to show Sam the proof, because I'm going on the road again tomorrow. Jerry Lee is doing the Steve Allen show July 28 and then a week later he'll be on the Alan Freed 'Big Beat' TV show. We'll spend the rest of the time calling on DJs and our distributors in New York and New Jersey.

"The exposure we get on these national shows will clinch Jerry Lee's career. When the whole country sees him, I predict that promoting Jerry Lee is going to take up most of my time the next few months. This fan mail's important, but it's just a drop in the bucket. There's a lot you could do to help us, girl. Not just Jerry Lee taking off like he has, but Johnny Cash needs our attention. Everything involved in this business is urgent. It's a fast business, and we have to keep up every single day. We have got to take hold of this situation. If we don't, it's going to swallow us." We had made our way to the front door when Jud, as an afterthought, asked, "Don't you want some iced tea or something before you take off in this heat?"

Mrs. Taylor's restaurant, with no musicians and just a couple of auto mechanics around, seemed strangely quiet. "So how do you think you're going to like the record business?" he said when his coffee and my tea arrived.

"I'm sort of intimidated," I answered. "I'm still trying to find out what Sun Records is all about."

"That could take some time," Jud admitted. "I've been with the company off and on since 1950 and there have been a lot of twists and turns, a lot of surprises, along the way. You'll learn just like we did—by experience. When we started making records, we didn't know anything. I knew there were some disk jockeys out there, but I didn't know their names or where they were. We knew there were places that would wholesale our records, but we didn't know who they were either, except the one in Memphis. We learned some hard lessons, too," he said, and his soft brown eyes took on a faraway look.

"But the company is really going well now, isn't it? How many hit records has Sun had in all?" I asked.

"Well, I can't give you a number, but aside from this thing going on with Jerry Lee, there have been enough to keep the doors open. The most unusual one was with a group we brought here from the Tennessee State Prison."

Just Walkin' in the Rain

He started to sing in a soft baritone, "Just walkin' in the rain, getting soaking wet. You've heard that, haven't you?"

"Yes, Johnnie Ray. I remember."

"No, Johnnie Ray covered it. It was our release first, with these five boys that Governor Frank Clement let us bring to Memphis to record. That was 1953 in the summer, and they were brought in shackles by some state guards. They called themselves 'The Prisonaires,'—people in Nashville knew about them. The governor was the kind of guy that was into music, and also public relations. He had them singing at functions up there, and they were pretty good, but of course being felons with long sentences, their career options were limited." He stared at me and smiled to be sure I caught the irony.

"But how many hits in all has Sun had?" I persisted.

"Well, that's what everybody wants, hit records, of course," Jud said. "But it takes some time to build an organization. Some of the sides Sam did with his blues artists had good sales in the R&B market, but most of those weren't on our label. The masters were leased to other labels. On Sun, Rufus Thomas had a hit with 'Bear Cat.' Sam released five singles on Elvis, from five sessions he had from '54 until '56, but we ran into promotion problems and all we got out of those were regional hits. But it gave Sam the chance to sell his contract on the basis of the stir he caused.

"This whole thing has exploded since Carl Perkins did 'Blue Suede Shoes.' Then Cash came on strong with 'Folsom Prison' and 'I Walk the Line.' Now Jerry Lee. Nothing like 'Whole Lot of Shakin'" has ever been played on pop radio. The girls go wild about him—he could be the biggest one of all. He looks different, he sings different, he *is* different. If I can just keep him on a leash." Jud gave a rueful laugh.

The conversation was fascinating, but as with Sam, there came a time when enough was enough. I thanked Jud for the iced tea and headed for the bus stop and Main Street, where Goldsmith's was advertising its new fall line. It was hot trying on winter clothes, but this was the time to get the best selection. I found a ruby-red jersey sheath with jacket that I thought would be a good color for me. I wagged the box it was packed in home on the bus along with the Jerry Lee photo that I had held onto with great care during my shopping trip.

And in the Afternoon

Katie from across the hall greeted me almost as soon as I put my key in the lock. She came bounding over from her apartment with two bottles in her hands. "Look what one of my listeners brought me," she said. "Gold and green Chartreuse." She was a DJ on Sam's radio station.

"What *is* that?"

"It's very expensive European liqueur," said this sophisticated transplant from San Francisco. "Want to try it?"

I got out a fruit-juice glass and poured about a jigger, turned it up and drank it in one swallow. Big mistake! I felt like I was on fire! It didn't help that I was already so hot from shopping and riding the bus in the heat.

"Thanks a lot! Why didn't you warn me? What does it have in it, pepper?"

Katie laughed and said, "You're supposed to sip it." She paused, and then said confidentially, "By the way. I believe I saw Sam Phillips leaving your apartment the other night as I was coming in. I just want you to know I'd never say anything about it to Becky." She gave me a sympathetic look.

She was referring to Sam's wife, who also worked at WHER. I hadn't met Becky yet, but Sam had spoken of her, one time saying he started the station for her so she would have something to do, and besides, she had some radio experience and a "damn nice voice." Katie's remark took me by surprise, and I didn't answer her. I was never good at comebacks, and I didn't think I needed to explain anything to her. Probably she wouldn't believe me anyway that these meetings were innocent.

I quickly excused myself and headed for the shower, thinking about the remarks made by some of the friends I'd made in my short while in Memphis. They seemed to think I was joining a fringy bunch of characters they wouldn't care to know. Was I going to be the topic of gossip, too? Then I thought, "People don't really care. They are thinking about themselves, so I have to do what's best for me."

The next time I saw Sam, I told him what Katie had said. It was the first time I'd seen him angry, and he had some choice uncomplimentary words to say about his employee, the tamest being that she was a phony. I was surprised he kept her on the job, since he said he hadn't liked her even before this incident. But I guess Sun kept him so busy he couldn't worry about personnel at WHER.

Finding Out about Fan Mail

Obviously, Jerry Lee, despite the critics who found him bordering on obscenity, had a rabid corps of fans, as I found when I started opening his mail. People were wild about "Whole Lot of Shakin'." Some letters and cards were scrawled in childish handwriting, others were typed and formal, none complained of dirty lyrics, and most wanted a picture. I started answering them on his new white stationery with black design and lettering. It featured the star's picture in the bottom corner with a rainbow-shaped cascade of music notes falling from the letterhead. I had asked Andy to specify sans serif type with no caps—very modern, I thought.

I would hand-address each envelope and write a greeting, like "Thanks for your letter and for listening. Best of luck (insert appropriate name)—Yours always, Jerry Lee Lewis." I tried to imitate his thin script signature with the prominent initial letters.

Sometimes I would pick up a stack of letters to answer at home, or occasionally I would answer them at the studio. Often a session would be going on, and I would have to wait in the front until the red light would go off and then it was OK to walk through the studio.

I was impressed by how big Sun was becoming in the entertainment industry. Jerry Lee was becoming known nationally not only because of his recordings, but through his appearances on the Steve Allen show and Dick Clark's *American Bandstand*. He had sung "Great Balls of Fire" and Carl Perkins had sung "Glad All Over" in the movie *Jamboree*, which wasn't in the Oscar league, but still, it was the movies!

Good Old Memphis Barbecue

One night a man I occasionally dated drove me by Sun to pick up the fan mail and came in to see the place. While I went to the back office, he chatted with Sam and Sally, and when I came back found out he'd asked them to come along with us for some barbecue at the Pig 'n' Whistle.

Jack, my date, was driving, and Sam and Sally were in the back seat. Making conversation, Jack asked Sam if he had any children, and Sam told him about his two boys, Knox and Jerry. They were about middle-school age then, very cute in the pictures Sam had shown, blond with ducktails. They were involved in soap-box derby, and obviously the pride of Sam's life. He went on a while in praise of them, and then he said, "But I always wanted a girl. I want to have a girl someday—by somebody."

Jack laughed and said, "Don't look at Barbara."

This remark of Sam's seemed offhand, but it made me wonder just what he had in mind in his relationship with Sally, who seemed to be everywhere Sam was.

Albums Hot Off the Press

Cold weather had come to Memphis, and I was looking forward to celebrating Thanksgiving with my mother for the first time since I went away to college. I had also been anticipating the arrival of the Cash and

Perkins albums, which were scheduled to be ready by mid-November. The welcome news came with a phone call from Regina, saying I could come to the office and pick up a copy. It was thrilling to see the long-play albums all finished with their labels and issue numbers, as well as the cover art and my writing on the back. I said to myself, "I have arrived. I guess I'm part of the record business now."

Sam came in just as I was leaving and asked me how I liked the albums. I told him I was stunned! This seemed like the big time. He said, "We needed to get that Cash album out now. The word about him is getting around. You know he was invited to the Grand Ole Opry this month. This will help us move some of those albums. I'm going to see a lot of DJs and distributors at the country music DJ convention this month, and you can be sure we'll create some excitement that way."

"Sit awhile, don't you want to?" he said, pointing to the loveseat. He had taken a seat at Regina's vacant desk. "You know, Barbara, this is what makes it all worthwhile. I like to discover talent. That is the greatest thing—to take somebody and help bring out the best they have to offer. If you had heard John Cash the first day he came in here, singing his little gospel songs, you or nobody else would have thought he'd turn into the star he has become in such a short time. Three big records, an album, and now the Opry. His dream. It's the greatest thing I could ever want to do." He went on again about how he had started his company to expose the world to the great talent in this region, to show people that their derogatory stereotypes of southerners—black and white—were false.

It was getting dark and I needed to catch my bus, so I had to forgo more philosophy from Sam, but I was indeed proud of him, and Johnny Cash, and even of me for writing these liner notes.

Decision Time

Off and on since summer, Sam had been asking me if I was ready to come to work full-time. One evening in early December, he came to my office while I was answering fan mail, sat down in the guest chair, and looked at me seriously. He explained that the load at the office was heavy and reiterated that Jud really needed backup in the office every day. Sam himself had other enterprises that demanded attention, and he couldn't give all of his efforts to the Sun business.

My excuses heretofore had been, I thought, valid, that I didn't feel I knew enough about the record business. That my mother insisted I not switch jobs before a year, because I'd resigned two others in a matter of months and that didn't look good on my résumé. I'd got the issue of an office for me solved, and Sam had even let me pick out a new Olivetti electric typewriter.

"I guess you'll think I'm being a little snobbish," I said, "but it really worries me about how dusty and untidy the studio is all the time." This might not bother some people, but it got to me every time I went in.

"Barbara, we have a cleaning service that comes in every Saturday. Things get disorganized after a session, but this place is basically easy to keep clean." He said it very seriously as if he truly understood that surroundings were important to me.

There was another, almost subconscious, reason I was a little wary of the Sun situation. I had noticed that Sam made no distinction between his personal and business life. He had never mentioned golf or fishing or other hobbies. He spent Sundays with his wife and boys, as far as I could tell. Otherwise, it seemed to be business or sleep, and he had a way of absorbing everyone into his routine. I wondered how it would work out, his being a night person and often not available in the daytime. It seemed Sally, Roy Scott, Jack, Bill, and Jud were in Sam's orbit, whatever the time. He had such charisma that people just got sucked into his wake, and perhaps he expected that. I valued my freedom and my private life, and I couldn't see building my life twenty-four hours a day around Sam Phillips. I was scared of him in a sort of psychological way.

I never even hinted at these thoughts to Sam, but he addressed them indirectly in our conversation. Sam was careful to reassure me that he was not interested in me personally. He said, "All those girls at WHER, I have never fooled with any of those girls. I want you to work for me because I love your mind. You have the best mind of any woman I have ever met. I believe in you. I believe in you more than you believe in yourself. I can tell you just a hint of what I want, and you can come up with exactly the right thing every time."

Of course I was flattered. I assured him that I appreciated his confidence and all he himself had done and stood for. "I know we could work together," I said. "I've just had to feel my way into this. Did you have a salary in mind?" I'd enjoyed the extra dollars my freelance work had brought in and hoped full-time work with Sun would give me a raise in salary.

Sam was willing to come up with ninety dollars a week, a bit more than I made at WMCT, and a very good salary at a time when the average woman worker was making fifty dollars a week. I would be giving up health and retirement benefits, but on one occasion Roy Scott had shown me a document about profit-sharing that Sam might set up. The most attractive lure was having some real work to do and more stimulating co-workers. "I hope you'll take it. I can't wait much longer or I'll have to start looking for someone else."

Sam fixed me with that gaze that could almost hypnotize, and I said, "I can start the first week in January. I'll give notice right away."

Making Plans

In deciding to work for Sam, I was going further afield from my original ambition of wanting to do TV news when I got my degree. I had learned almost as soon as I graduated from college that this door was shut tight for women. I had had other media jobs, but chances for advancement were almost nonexistent. I was about ready to give up on life in the business world.

Therefore, during the time I'd been doing the part-time work for Sam, I had also been formulating some long-range plans for myself. They began to take shape when I read a brief news story in the *Memphis Commercial Appeal*. The article said an impending explosion in the numbers of entering college freshmen was going to require many more college teachers. I had liked college, especially the annual rhythm of work and vacations. I began to imagine myself some years hence, married, I hoped. If I were a teacher, I could work and also be home in early afternoons and summers to enjoy family life. I had investigated the local university, Memphis State, and found out I could get an MA in English through night and Saturday study. Then I could be ready when the baby boomers arrived.

In taking the job with Sun, I was thinking I could work several or many years, depending on how my career progressed with Sam and what developed in my life.

Getting to Memphis State, however, would require a car. Even with the small raise, the only way to save money would be to give up my apartment. Conveniently, my mother had found a nice widow who would rent me a room. At the time I gave notice to WMCT, I also gave notice to my landlord, gave away my few household furnishings, and soon moved in with a lady in an apartment who promised to give me a continental breakfast and a ride to the studio on the way to her work downtown.

When I went home for Christmas vacation, my mind was at ease with these plans. In the spirit of making new starts, on January 5, 1958, I took another leap and was confirmed in the Episcopal Church by Bishop Barth at St. Mary's Cathedral. I offered my first communion for the healing of Knox Phillips, Sam's son, who was very ill in the hospital, and about whom Sam had expressed great concern.

TWO

EARLY 1958

Ooby Dooby

ROY ORBISON (SUN 242)

I Am Now an Official Employee

The next day, which was January 6, 1958, I went to work for Sun Records, and I was feeling pretty confident. I had already gotten familiar with my office during the six months I had freelanced, and I had gotten to know Sam, Jud, and Sally and had met Jack Clement a couple of times. Sam had given me a key to the door in case I needed to open up. When I arrived I was happy to see Sun's receptionist, Regina Reese, already sitting at her desk, all fresh and perky.

Regina, like Elvis, was from Tupelo but she was a couple of years younger than he was. Her voice dripped honey. Though she was petite, she seemed taller because of her ramrod posture and three-inch heels. She welcomed me and said we could go for coffee after a while, but asked if I wanted to see the folder of letters and phone messages she had been collecting for someone to deal with. "These are from last week, but I think Sam would want you to take care of them." She explained that Sam wasn't coming in because Knox was still in the hospital and Sam was there with him. Sally would be in after ten, but her duties involved invoices, bookkeeping, and payroll. Sam had said everything else would go to me.

On my way to my office, I encountered a person I'd not seen before, a stout teenager with a ruddy complexion who was singing and yodeling a country song to herself. She stopped singing at the sight of me and said in a commanding voice, "I've got a job for you." She obviously knew I was the new employee.

I told her my name and asked her what she wanted me to do. Pointing to a square cardboard box sitting on a table, she said these 45 records needed to be placed in some individual mailing wrappers and labeled. "They need to be done right away because Doug is coming by after lunch to take them to the post office."

I had never seen or heard of this person, or Doug either, but I was sure Sam hadn't hired me to pack records. I was thinking of what to say when she continued abruptly, "You can stand over here."

"I don't think I can do that," I countered. "I need to go to my office and try to answer this correspondence for Sam."

I took the folder to my office and began puzzling over the little pink phone message slips. The names were sometimes followed by call letters of radio stations, but otherwise they held few clues about why I needed to call them. Within an hour, Regina came back to the office with another sheaf of papers, that day's mail, which she had opened but was passing on to me. Some of it was fan mail, one type of letter I knew what to do with.

"Who is that in the studio?" I asked.

Regina said, "That's Kay Keisker. She's related to the lady who was here before you, Marion Keisker."

I told her Kay seemed to resent my reluctance to help her. Regina laughed, "That's just Kay. She even tries to get the musicians to pack records. She's OK. Don't worry."

Some of the letters I read that day requested sample copies for small stations not on Sun's mailing list. I took the letters to Kay, who grunted and pointed for me to "put them there." Some of the calls or letters from distributors were equally simple—orders for records. They ranged from orders of thousands of Jerry Lee Lewis or Johnny Cash releases to long lists of one or two copies of numbers from Sun's extensive back catalog.

One of the first things I learned that first week was how to call in orders to the pressing plants—Plastic Products of Memphis for states in the South and Midwest, Paramount in Philadelphia for the East Coast, and Monarch in Los Angeles for the West. I returned some of the calls and was either able to handle their business or take a complete message for Sam or Jud. For example, some distributors were requesting authorization to return records. I started a new file folder called "Ask Sam" and then went up front to see if it was time for coffee.

The Musicians Are Coming!

People were starting to arrive. Billy Riley, a striking black-haired young man, walked in and asked Regina if he had any mail or phone calls. She said sweetly, "I don't think so, Billy." I assumed he was a staff member, but Regina said, "No, he plays guitar on a lot of sessions, but he comes in most days just to see if anything is happening." He proceeded to make a couple of phone calls as if this were his place of business.

Billy suggested we go for coffee next door to Taylor's Restaurant. We did, and Jimmy Wilson, who I learned was an eccentric session pianist who lived upstairs over the restaurant, joined us. Not inclined toward small talk, he put some money in the jukebox and played "Fraulein" by Bobby Helms. Soon he was lost in the story: "I love that song, man, but it's so sad. Just think of that GI—probably didn't even speak good German." He gazed out the window at the traffic going by on Union Avenue, lost in misery over that ill-fated love affair. His mood matched the weather, which was gray, cold, and threatening rain. Suddenly coming back to the present, Jimmy informed us, "Gotta split, man," and headed out the door.

"Weird dude, man," said Billy Riley. "Has a gun collection upstairs and sometimes he won't come down for sessions because he gets too wrapped up in playing with his guns. He's a pretty good musician and he knows sound. He put tacks in the piano keys to give a sort of percussion sound to his playing." He added that Wilson was one of his Little Green Men, the name of his band in homage to the public's fascination with a possible Martian invasion at that time. They had even recorded a song called "Flyin' Saucers Rock 'n' Roll."

Regina added with a little laugh, "Last week Jimmy Wilson introduced me to this chick he said was his wife. Two weeks before that, there was a different one, and he said *that* was his wife. He told Bill Justis he got rid of the other one because she was a sloppy housekeeper." After that, Regina and I would speculate about how many wives any new musician might have.

"Yeah, he also had a pet raccoon, but he decided it was too much trouble, so he took a hammer to its head," Riley replied. I decided I'd steer clear of Jimmy Wilson.

I asked Billy how he happened to get involved in making records. He said, "I was playing in a little country band in Arkansas and one Christmas Eve when I was driving from Jonesboro to Nettleton to see my mother, I see these two guys hitchhiking, and it turns out to be Jack Clement and Slim Wallace. Slim's band had been playing a dance, too, and Jack was the singer. Also played guitar and mandolin. Their car had broke down on the way home. I told them I was going just a few miles, but they were welcome to go that far.

"We got to talking about music, and I kept going till I had brought them all the way to Memphis. I guess that was my lucky night, you know, or unlucky, ha ha. Slim and Jack were partners in Fernwood Records, and they tried recording me. They had to take the tapes to Sam to be mastered, and then Sam bought the records and gave me a contract. After that, Jack came to work here. So Jack and me, we've been doing stuff with Sam ever since."

Regina made a signal it was time to get back, because we'd locked up when we left and shouldn't be away from the phones too long.

The "Raunchy" Man

But when we got back, Bill Justis had come in and was sitting at Sally's desk. I recognized him from the picture that was used in the Phillips International brochure, but when Regina introduced us, I could see that this Bill was not the serious one of his photo and certainly not "Raunchy," as in the song that made his name famous in rock 'n' roll circles.

"Bill, this is Barbara. She's come to work with us," Regina said in a very kind and pleased way, as if it were entirely her wonderful idea.

Bill rose from his seat and leaned over the desk to shake my hand. "Yeah. Groovy. How're you doing? Come to join the squirrels, huh?" With this his eyebrows shot up and he gave Regina a knowing look.

"I'm glad to meet you, Bill. I know about you because I wrote the blurb about you in the Phillips brochure," I said.

"Oh, yeah? You did that? Right." With that, he sat back down at Sally's desk, where he continued writing on some music composition paper. The overall impression Bill gave was one of civility and roundness. His face was round and almost glowed, sort of like the man in the moon, an effect enhanced by his shiny bald pate and wide smile. His entire shape and his tummy were softly curved, but in a likable way.

Back in my office, I was concentrating hard on the mail when the door opened and I saw Jack Clement peering inside. "What are you doing back here?" he asked.

"Do you mean right this minute, or do you mean what am I supposed to be doing, like all the time?" I responded.

"Whichever," he said, so I told him my job was to try to sell records, to the public and to our distributors. How I'd do that remained to be seen.

"OK, cool," he said. "If you need anything, I'm right next door."

I could hear him walk the few steps back to the control room, and occasionally I'd hear some squeaking sounds that told me he was working with tapes.

Getting Connected

Rooting around in the office, I found a box of cards, each of which had the call letters of a radio station and the names of DJs or program directors. "I might as well start somewhere," I thought and picked a card, intending to ask some of the radio people how Jerry Lee's "Great Balls of Fire" was going with their listeners. It had been released in November, and in December Sun had shipped one million copies. It had reached #2 on the *Billboard* pop chart, #3 in R&B, and #1 in country, as well as #1 in Britain's pop chart. Sam wanted to keep it going as long as possible, and in fact the record did continue to sell a long time. It remained on the charts for over four months, which made it a fabulous hit and money-maker for Sun and Jerry Lee.

In a general way I had known about record "top 100" lists, but their importance was stressed to me in my earliest contact with Sun. They not only were a barometer of a record's success, and that of the manufacturer, but the charts could help make or break a new record with their "pick of the week" spotlights. They were a self-enforcing form of promotion. *Billboard* magazine had pop charts, country charts, local market charts, a variety of other charts having to do with sales, plus airplay and jukebox play—and being on these charts was the name of the game. *Cashbox* and *Music Reporter* in Nashville also had influential charts. Getting a record noticed as a "pick" in one of these magazines could greatly influence airplay and sales, so one of my jobs was to cultivate the trade-publication people and watch those charts.

For my debut phone call as a record promoter, I decided to start at the top and selected radio station WERE in Cleveland. When I identified myself, I was put through immediately to the man I had been told by Jud was the biggest jock in that market or, for rock 'n' roll, in the entire United States—Bill Randle. Everyone in the industry courted him. Just as I said my name but before I could get into my pitch about Jerry Lee, he said, "Gotta go, on the air."

That was not too encouraging, but I selected a couple of other names at random and got a better response to my calls. The guys I called were playing the Jerry Lee record, and the fans loved it. I was thinking, "This is more fun than work." Up to now, calling long-distance had been a pretty big deal for me. I'd only done it about a dozen times and received about that same number of long-distance calls in my lifetime. I felt sort of omnipotent sitting there with those cards and that phone and just ringing up anybody I chose. The Phillips International line (JAckson 7-7291) was like my personal phone. The public knew the Sun phone

(JAckson 7-7216), and it was the one everyone usually rang in on. The next few days I accumulated a pretty good list of jocks I'd called. I also placed calls to all our forty-two distributors to introduce myself and discuss our recent releases and a few of the back numbers like "Raunchy" that were still selling well.

Without exception, all the big DJs were male, and all those on my call list were also white. All of our distributors were male and, incidentally, there was only one black distributor. He was in Chicago. Likewise their promotion people, except a woman in Dallas named Alta Hayes. Sam liked to phone her himself. She had helped break Elvis's early records in Texas, and Sam had great loyalty to her. Other than Alta and Frances Preston of the publishing-licensing group Broadcast Music Inc., in Nashville, it seemed the entire record business was male. I did hear of one of the majors having a woman publicist, but these big companies were so remote from us that I didn't know for sure if there was one or if there were several out there.

Every so often, I would go up front and talk with Regina and that day's drop-ins. Sometimes Jack would be on Regina's phone lining up "pickers," as he called them, for sessions. His phone list and session schedule stayed on her desk. In time I noticed Sam shared this desk, too, when he was in. At lunchtime we would go to Taylor's Restaurant or farther down the street to a little café that had a good vegetable-plate special. It was all novel, very entertaining to be soaking up the atmosphere, learning the language of the record business. But what I really wanted to do was talk to Sam, ask questions and tell him what I'd been doing. Knox was doing better and expected to go home any day, but still no Sam.

A constant stream of people dropped by, most of them wanting to see Sam. Almost every day one or more scared-looking hillbilly types with their guitars would come in and say they wanted to audition for Sam. Sometimes Bill or Jack would listen to the hopefuls if they weren't too busy or were in the mood. Songwriters seemed to be in great supply. Some would stay all morning, like a man named Floyd Huddleston, who was identified as a veteran of Glenn Miller's band and a close friend of Johnny Mercer's. We thought he was way square, but I was impressed when I heard he had written "Swanee River Rock," a big hit recorded in the Sun studio for the popular Mississippi college band, the Red Tops. He had a recording studio in Memphis that made commercial jingles, the pits for a musician, but a place singers and players could go to make a few bucks.

Others would come and go, not even asking to play their songs, just passing the time. Some business types came by hoping to sell Sam their wares or services—a diamond merchant; the Western Union guy; the account executive, Bill, from Union Planters Bank. Mitt Addington was a songwriter-psychologist who wanted to write and record for us and also contract to provide mental health services for any and all on the staff. Wonder why he thought we needed that? The numbers of people and their infinite variety were amazing, especially since so few visits resulted in any transaction. The ones who knew I had a private office would sometimes come there to sit and wait, invited or not. I kept hoping one day that Elvis would be among them. I still hadn't seen him or any of the other stars except Bill Justis.

I saw the illustrious Dewey Phillips (no relation to Sam) early in my days at Sun, but I didn't know who he was. He was in the control room with Jack and one of the sidemen, playing the Lonnie Johnson record of "Tomorrow Night" and singing along. He also had brought in some Lonnie Donegan and skiffle singers records, and I stopped in to listen to them along with the others. I wasn't introduced, but Jack Clement told me later how Dewey had been the first DJ to play an Elvis recording on the air, in 1954. Dewey at that time had a popular show called "Red, Hot, and Blue" on WHBQ radio and had introduced "That's All Right, Mama." Dewey's listeners went wild over the King's records, flooding the switchboard with calls, so Dewey located Elvis at a movie house and ordered him to come right over for his first radio interview. That's how Elvis was launched.

A Nickname and an Amusing Proposal

Toward the middle of the week, I was beginning to feel frustrated. Still no Sam. Almost every day musicians would be in the studio playing, sometimes rehearsing tunes with our unofficial "house band"; other times, Jack might be having a session with musicians I didn't recognize. Back in my office, I could hear and almost feel through the walls the bass going "thump, thump," a sound that got integrated into my nervous system through my years at Sun. There wasn't much drinking during the daytime, but often I could tell from the wastebaskets in the morning that there were some festive night sessions going on.

It was after one of these that Regina and I came in one morning to find Jack Clement looking disheveled and obviously drunk, having spent the entire night with the musicians in the studio. The other guys had left, but Jack was sitting at Sally's desk and in the mood to talk. He and Regina had dated before I came to Sun, so their relationship was sometimes a little edgy. She looked at him warily as he talked of one thing and another, occasionally pausing to sing a phrase of a song. He had a tic that made one of his eyes blink off and on. Then he addressed me.

"Barbara Barnes," he said. He said it again. "B.B. That's your name, I'm going to call you B.B," and then he started to muse about what he wanted to do that day. We were paying half-attention until he said what he wanted to do was have sex. But he hated to get all cleaned up, call a girl, take her out, and go through all that routine. He just wanted to have sex.

I hadn't heard a guy speak his thoughts quite so bluntly before, but Regina and I both just nodded. Then he looked at me and said, "Do you ever wake up horny? Wait—let me give you my phone number." He tore a little pink slip from Sally's phone pad and wrote down his phone number. "You can call me any morning. Just call that number."

I said, "Thank you, Jack."

Then he got up and left. We didn't hear of any accidents or arrests, so we assumed he made it home to sleep it off. By late afternoon he was back, refreshed, ready to get back at the task of finding songs and talent, making recordings like a good A&R man.

The Natives Get Restless

The next day Jack hadn't called a session, and only Regina, Kay, and I were there. But some musicians I was beginning to recognize as regulars came in about noon to practice. With Jack not there, they weren't too focused and they had some beer and Thunderbird wine. The music was getting louder and happier as the afternoon wore on.

The drummer was J. M. Van Eaton, the youngest of the group, a short, innocent-faced young man with a blond crewcut. He had started at Sun when he was too young to drive, and Billy Riley had to pick him up for sessions. J.M. was sort of hazing me, playing a marching-band beat when I walked through the studio. Martin Willis, the sax player, would laugh when J.M. did that, but I would march on pretending not to notice. Roland Janes, who played guitar and bass, had taken a dislike to me at first glance and wasn't friendly. During my second day at work he was sitting on the loveseat when he looked up and said defiantly, "You don't need to look at me like that. I bet I've got more money than you have." I must have been in another world, because I hadn't been thinking of him or even aware I was looking at him. I was too stunned to say anything, but Regina gave a little laugh and exclaimed, "Roland!" He was right, though. He no doubt had more money than I did.

Billy Riley was there as usual. I had been struck by the way he jutted out his chin on the beat, like a cobra about to strike. Most musicians nodded or patted their feet. That day, however, he decided to forsake the group to visit my little office to inform me that he was just the special one who was going to take out this new chick. He was obviously happy drunk when he came bouncing acrobatically into my office. He had the beautiful high cheekbones, dark complexion, and gleaming black hair of one of his Cherokee ancestors. In fact, that day I could see in him a wild Indian, muscular, compact, and untamed.

"You are going out with me tonight," he announced. "You are going to say, 'I never had as good a time as I did when I went out with Billy Riley.'"

"I don't think that's such a good idea, Billy," I said. He was charming and funny as he kept elaborating on how he really knew how to show a girl a good time. After a while, the thought dawned on him that I really wasn't going to accept and he left, but he didn't seem crushed.

The last hour before five went slowly, but I had found enough work to do setting up some artist files, and at closing time I walked to the front just minutes before Kay Keisker, who had to share her shipping space in the studio with the musicians, came through the door crying. She said that one of the guys had molested her. Regina and I tried to soothe her and find out what had happened, but she was incoherent. I told Kay to go sit down next door and then go home. With the musicians, I had had enough.

I opened the door to the studio and said in my most authoritative voice, "Everybody out. I'm closing the studio." The musicians looked at me, and J.M. hit a lick on the snare and then the cymbal. "I mean it, leave," I commanded. They looked from one to the other and then back at me. "You have to get out," I said. "Right now."

They actually got up and left. When the last one was gone, Regina got out her key to lock up, and she said, "B.B., you were magnificent."

After these initial incidents, I was accepted as one of the gang, and I began to become friends with the musicians and to enjoy seeing, hearing, and talking with them.

Getting Down to Serious Business

During that week when I was being initiated into the daily workings of Sun, I was speaking with Jud daily. I asked him if it would be helpful to have daily sales records to let him know what was selling and who was buying. He said, "yes," so I asked Regina if she could start tabulating the invoices each day and mailing them to Jud on the road, giving me a carbon.

She was busy answering phones all day as well as typing a backlog of trip reports Jud had been dictating over the phone. These were his weekly highlights concerning distributor relations, promotion efforts, and so forth. Sam and I both needed to have this information, but Sam particularly needed the financial information. Regina handed over an accumulation of these for me to read as part of my orientation. Here are a few passages I found especially interesting: "I flew into one of the worst snowstorms you will ever see, going from Boston to Buffalo. Women screaming, weaving up and down the aisles, children throwing up. The plane was lurching every which way and I didn't know if we were going to land right side up or upside down. From Buffalo I went to Cleveland and at Cleveland you turned me around and sent me on to Albany."

In reading these, I learned not only about the weather, but also of some of the unscrupulous and illegal practices that cropped up in the record industry, as in another Jud report: "This information I received regarding his (distributor's) putting three or four presses in his place of business seems to be verified from sources that are reputable, so it would pay us to watch out for bootleg records."

The industry consensus was that about a third of all singles sold in the United States at that time were from illegal operations like this. Bootlegging was one of the reasons performers were correct in alleging they didn't get all the royalties due them, even though their record label may have been reporting all sales.

In determining how credit-worthy distributors might be, Jud would often dig up detailed information about prospective or current associates. One example that I found very interesting concerned one distributor who sold to retailers called record rack jobbers. These merchants would stock an assortment of current releases on vertical racks in different types of stores. According to Jud, "He went from Philadelphia with MGM Records to open up the trade when there was no distributor there at all and he and his brother-in-law have formed several corporations. He owns one/half of 37 1/2 percent of the capital stock in the record rack business with the proviso that he has control as to what merchandise is to be put on the racks, therefore protecting the lines that he has in his distributorship. He went into the record rack business to maintain control over the RCA operation and has brought pressure to bear on his manufacturers not to sell to record racks that merchandise through the 5&10 cent stores. As a result he has almost completely put them out of business in that area."

These reports of Jud's helped me understand what it meant to do business on a national scale and to find out what I needed to know about the individual businesses I was dealing with daily. Each market had a point value—such as 3.5—which was supposed to be a gauge of what percentage of our business we could expect to glean there. Of course, it didn't work, because there were so many variables of regional tastes, methods of getting exposure, per capita income in the area, and others.

I enjoyed Jud's phone calls. He not only had an intimate and musically expressive voice, but he also surprised me with his colorful language, spiced with country metaphors. One day, complaining about the competitive atmosphere he was running into, he said plaintively, "It's as rough as a cob out here." I quoted him to my landlady, and she told me that way back when corn cobs were used in privies instead of toilet paper, that metaphor expressed the idea of real pain.

Grease and Mud

That's what Bill Justis called the fare at our next-door hangout, Taylor's Restaurant. Among the questions I raised when Sam was talking about hiring me concerned the lack of places to eat in the neighborhood. As time went on, I found out that Mrs. Taylor's was it for food, and the Sun clientele could have kept it in business. Modest though it was with its Formica-topped booths, bare tables, and Naugahyde seating, it was like an adjunct office where staff could socialize and Sam could talk business. Bill Justis sat there alone to write lead sheets. Mrs. Dell Taylor, who somehow brought to mind the worldly wise pub keepers in British movies, was happy for us to stay as long as we cared to.

Most everyone just had coffee there in the morning, but Jack, Sam, and Sally ate breakfast there almost every day. Fresh eggs cooked over easy in bacon grease sat proudly on the white plates beside a generous serving of bacon or sausage patties. Buttered toast could be spread with jam from the jars on the tables. Rosemary, Mrs. Taylor's daughter, came around with refills for our coffee and was cheerful and friendly, especially with the musicians.

Lunchtime the tables filled up with mechanics and salesmen from nearby automobile row, while our little crowd claimed the booths by the window. At noon, the place buzzed with talk, drowning out the jukebox, and the air grew hazy with cigarette smoke. I ate lunch there most days, usually ordering vegetable soup or the sirloin strip. Soup was less than a dollar and the steak about two dollars. Mrs. Taylor kept our tabs in a box under the counter. Every so often I would ask her to see how much I owed and I would write her a check for five or six dollars.

Sam's Here!

Friday came, and the long-awaited event arrived! The white Cadillac pulled up at the curb about ten o'clock and Sam bounced out. He was obviously in a very good mood, appearing fit and energetic—a man in his prime with his thirty-fifth birthday just a few days past. He was wearing a brown tweed jacket and pleated pants, with his luxuriant brown hair growing longer for winter, sort of like kittycats do, I thought. His buoyancy affected other people—sort of made them perk up, and everyone wanted his attention. This adulation inspired him to strut a bit, I came to notice in future days, when he sometimes referred to himself as "Sambo Slick."

That Friday we "girls" had only a moment to say "hello" before one of the people waiting around, Bill Decker, grabbed him. Bill managed WHER, and off they went to Mrs. Taylor's café to talk radio business. When Bill left, it was Bill Justis's turn, and then Sam got on the phone, receiving and placing a stream of calls. Then Sam and Sally went to lunch next door, and during the afternoon he and Jack were in the control room talking and listening to tapes.

About five o'clock I went up front, still wondering when I would be able to edge my way in. When he finally turned his attention to me, I showed him my manila folder where I'd been keeping papers I needed to ask him about, and he said, "We need to go somewhere quiet so we can look at all that." With a gesture, he indicated for everyone in the room to come along.

Roy Scott, who had come in just before I approached Sam, held the door for Regina to come out with him. Sally locked up and headed with Sam and Regina for the Cadillac. I had been eyeing Roy Scott's cute little green MG and asked if I could ride with him. Our two-car procession ended not far away at a Travelodge Motel. Sam let us into a room with a key from his pocket. He took out a bottle of J&B from a paper bag, sent Sally for some ice, and proceeded to pour everyone a Scotch and water, except for Sally, who didn't drink.

Almost before we had sat down, Sam started talking. He seemed to have a lot of thoughts stored up waiting to be expressed. Occasionally he would direct a remark at Roy, who entered into conversation with him, or to Sally, but mostly it was stream of consciousness. I had learned in an earlier meeting that Sam had actually preached at a church in Alabama. Later it came out that he had also had an ambition to be a lawyer as well as preacher. He had of course been a radio announcer. Oratory was his forte, it seemed; he certainly liked to hear himself talk.

I tried to interject something about the papers in my folder once or twice, but after a while gave in to the slow, warming effect of the Scotch, relaxing my spine lower in the armchair, just listening to the evangelistic cadences of Sam's rhetoric. It was like listening to music or a foreign language. The rationality of it just wasn't entirely connecting in my brain. I could have slipped deeper into that pleasant state with more Scotch, given my fatigue after that first exciting week on the job, but I came to myself after a couple of hours and thought it was a good idea to go home. No one seemed to notice as I dialed the desk clerk to order a cab. In a few minutes, I walked out on the sidewalk, motioning to Regina that she could come with me if she wished. She did.

On the way home, I asked her, "Is this a usual type of thing, Regina?"

"Pretty much," she said.

The previous times I'd been around Sam in the evening were businesslike, and work was involved. This was a different, much more intimate scene, and this Sam was one I hadn't seen before. On my various jobs, I had made it a point never to mingle much with co-workers and especially bosses on a social level. The pitfalls were obvious. I hoped I would be able to stick to that policy in this new job with no hard feelings.

Hometown Visit

The next morning I traveled the ninety miles to my hometown, Corinth, Mississippi, by Trailways bus. The eight o'clock wasn't crowded, so I curled up over an entire two-seat space near the driver. The gray, bare woods and fields sped by along Highway 72. The landscape looked dismal, the other passengers forlorn. The fumes from the engine had seeped into the bus so long that the interior was saturated with the smell of burning gas. I couldn't wait for the day when I could afford a car.

Soon I was walking into Mother's warm and cheery apartment, which dispelled the gloom with its rose-colored sofa and draperies, flowered chair, and all the little treasures of her life. I could feel myself growing younger and lighter in the glow of her motherly pleasure of having me home. It was so good to be in a safe place where I was totally known and totally welcome. A beef roast was in the oven, and a coconut cake sat on a cut-glass cake plate.

After lunch I walked down Fillmore Street to WCMA radio, bursting to tell my friends there about my new job. Johnny Bell, the manager, had given me my first job doing a weekly high-school news and music show when I was sixteen. That was unpaid, but I got some training, and later Johnny paid me pretty well in the summers while I was in college for reporting local news and doing a daily show on the air.

Johnny and Joe Van Dyke, the sales manager, seemed surprised when I popped into Johnny's office, but pleased with my news about Sun. At last, someone who knew about Sun Records and thought I'd made a good move! Most everyone I knew in Memphis had only a vague notion of what Sun was, and some of my friends were mystified by my decision to go to work there. They were into J. D. Salinger and West Coast jazz, and Sun's music was not to their taste.

Johnny said, "I don't know Sam Phillips, but I've known about him a long time through radio connections. Our friend Buddy Bain knew those guys like Elvis and Roy Orbison, because his band used to play with them when they did shows all around this area." He was referring to a WCMA country DJ who had left the station the previous year to be on TV in nearby Tupelo, Mississippi, Elvis's hometown.

"Elvis used to drop by here and Buddy would teach him guitar licks. I think he used to stay with Buddy some," Johnny said.

Joe chimed in, "And, you know, Carl Perkins's wife, Valda, is from Corinth. Carl and his brothers played for years in all the joints around

North Mississippi and West Tennessee. I heard those Perkins boys were pretty rough. He had a show on WTJS back when (referring to WCMA's sister station in Jackson, Tennessee). Have you met Elvis and Carl yet?"

"I haven't met many of the big artists yet, but I have seen Elvis. Last summer he was riding along Main Street in Memphis in a purple Cadillac convertible. I was upstairs at an Alvin Roy exercise club, and I looked down and there was Elvis with a bunch of guys.

"It was here in Corinth I saw him closer up, though, about 1954 or '55 when I was home from college. One time when he was playing the courthouse, I saw him riding around with Shirley Drewry and her sister. He was wearing a pink-and-black outfit. We thought he was a real greaser." Those girls were not in my same grade in school, and I didn't really know them, but the Drewry name in Corinth was associated with gambling, bootlegging, and prostitution. Elvis's choice of company made me have doubts about him.

"That was before he became so famous," I added. "I understand he comes by the studio every time he comes to Memphis, but it's always at night, so I don't guess I'll be seeing him there."

Joe Van Dyke ironically noted, "Nobody in Memphis will be seeing him before long, now that the draft board says he's 1A. He'll be off to the Army pretty soon."

Johnny Bell changed the subject, asking, "Do you know who came here looking for an announcing job? Johnny Cash. I turned him down. Tommy Weaver was in the Air Force with him in Germany and gave him my name for when he got out of service. He had an Arkansas accent so thick, no one could understand him. He couldn't read a thirty-second spot in a minute. I told him if he wanted to be in radio, he should get some training at Keegan radio school in Memphis. He and Tommy were together in a communications unit, so I guess he had a little technical knowledge of radio already." Tommy was one of Johnny Bell's other protégés who got a start at WCMA when he was in high school.

"I understand he did go to Keegan for awhile," I chimed in.

Joe said, "I hear Sam Phillips is quite the ladies' man."

"Oh, I don't think that's true. Just the opposite. He's so proud of his wife and boys. I've been around him several months, and he's never hit on me, never made any suggestive remarks. I think that must be just a rumor." Joe didn't respond except to raise his eyebrows a little.

"I guess you've met Jud Phillips, haven't you? I've heard stories about that man," Johnny said. "Do you remember Bill Jobe, who used to write for *The Corinthian*? He told me a story about how Jud Phillips started a riot at one of Elvis's first concerts outside of the South while he was managing Elvis. It was either in Pittsburgh or Philadelphia, I forget which, but in Pennsylvania. Elvis was booked for three shows and at the first one, 300 fans showed up in a 10,000-seat building. For the second show, Jud took 2,000 tickets and gave them, along with two dollars, to every young girl he found on the street. He promised that there would be a prize for the one who could steal the most of Elvis's clothes after the concert. Well, you should have seen the mob! Elvis's clothes were shredded. Word got around, and the third show sold out. The Associated Press picked up the story, and that was Elvis's first national publicity." I could believe Jud did that, even from the short time I had known him.

I soon left the radio men to their work, walking down the familiar steep steps and out into the crisp air. I took my time, squashing with my heels the acorns strewn about and avoiding the big cracks in the sidewalks where the roots of giant trees had buckled the concrete. I passed the big house where first the Confederate and then the Federal generals had stayed around the time of the Battle of Shiloh, the little Presbyterian and Episcopal churches, the tall Baptist steeple rising above the white church, and the friendly houses of people whose names I knew.

Back to Work on Monday

As much as I enjoyed my restorative weekend, I could hardly wait to get back to Sun on Monday to see what was going to happen next. Jack Clement and Regina were already there when I arrived, and I confessed to them my confusion and difficulty getting the hang of things at Sun. "There doesn't seem to be any order here," I said. "I never know what to expect."

"That's it, B.B. And you never will. I used to feel that way, but you have to go with it, relax. Just look upon it as your own three-ring circus," Jack advised.

Regina had been listening, at the same time opening the mail. In the stack of letters she found and handed to me a little flat package that turned out to hold a nice surprise. It was a type of recording I had never seen before—a small square laminated cover holding a regular-looking 45 record, but with two tunes on each side. It was what they called an Extended Play album, or EP. This one was from our European partner, London Records.

The flexible plastic cover had an orange background and showed a fellow lounging on a haystack, with the title *Hillbilly Rock*. The singer, Roy Orbison, was one of the guys who played shows in the mid-South with our other artists, so he was in town often and came to hang around occasionally. The next time he showed up, I was eager to let him see it. To my surprise, he wasn't thrilled with his release.

"I don't like that cover too much," he said softly. He had had a country-and-western band at home in West Texas, but being depicted as a hillbilly offended his dignity. He represented the western part of country-western music, and he had changed his band's name from the Wink Westerners to the Teen Kings, in hopes of becoming a rock star. He had grown up more urbanized, and he'd been to college.

"But Roy, this means you are popular enough in Europe to warrant this EP. You should be happy. The liner notes were very complimentary." I didn't add that they had termed Roy a "rock-a-billy," a term I hadn't heard before but one that did seem to reflect the way Sun's music owed something to hillbilly, something to rock 'n' roll.

The featured tune was "Ooby Dooby," one of his four Sun releases thus far and his biggest hit. It was described as an up-tempo rock 'n' roll number that had nonsense lyrics. The rhyming title reminded me of Little Richard's "Tutti Frutti," and songs like these were a reason that condescending critics said rock 'n' roll was juvenile.

"'Ooby Dooby' was a good record," Roy had to admit. "It was #59 on the *Billboard* pop charts and sold a quarter of a million records."

Roy liked the feeling of having a successful record, and he was impatient for another. Instead of goofing around or shooting the breeze with Billy Riley or the other guys, he seemed to be working when he came in, sitting in the studio playing his guitar, at times just sitting and thinking, writing down a line or two, or occasionally coming into my office to talk about his career aspirations. He seemed very focused on success and was frustrated Sam wasn't paying more attention to him. On the day we were looking at his EP, he seemed friendly and inclined to chat, so I asked him for a favor.

"Roy, I need to stop by the printer's for a minute. If I catch the bus, it will take me all morning. Would you mind driving me there and back if you have time?" I asked.

He said he would and very politely opened the door for me to climb into his sleek, finned white Cadillac. I was thinking, "By the looks of this car, he's doing pretty well. Why isn't he happy?"

"This is a really comfortable car, Roy," I said. "You must be very proud of it."

He replied, "This is my 'Ooby Dooby' car. When I bought it I thought I could afford it. Last year I made $50,000 but by the way things are going now, I'll be lucky if I make $3,000 this year. I've had one release since 'Ooby Dooby' and I don't have much hope for it." He said it with a sense of despair, as if fearing that his luck might never change. The odd tune that Bill Justis had written for him, "Chicken Hearted," seemed like a loser to me, too. Roy's voice sounded thin and had a little quaver on this one, and I didn't like the lyrics. Neither did Roy.

"How did you get to Sun?" I asked.

"Well, the long way around, I guess. I found out about Sun when I saw Elvis in Dallas in 1954," he said. "I was doing country at the time, but when he sang 'Maybellene,' the crowd went wild." Roy said he decided he wanted a crowd to respond to him that way, and that's why he came to Memphis. In effect, he wanted to be the next Elvis. Roy dropped me off at the studio and glided away in his big machine. When I had a chance to talk with Jack Clement, I asked him about Roy.

"It took a while for Sam to get interested in him, but he has hopes for Roy as an artist and especially as a songwriter. He likes his picking, too. When he and his girlfriend Claudette came to town, Sam and

Becky put them up for awhile." Jack added that Sam sometimes found it frustrating to work with Roy, because he didn't sing loud enough and was always bugging them with these ballads he wanted to sing. "Sam wants everybody to stick with rock 'n' roll. That's what's commercial," Jack concluded.

Roy had a bit of an identity problem when it came to rock, because he wanted to be a star like Elvis, but he didn't have that love for R&B that came out in the music of Elvis, Carl Perkins, Jerry Lee, and others. Maybe he hadn't drunk enough Mississippi River water growing up.

"But Sam likes Roy. One time they were having a session and Roy's band walked out on him. I would have thought Sam would blow up about that, but he just told Roy to forget it, there were other bands."

Listening later to the four tunes on the EP, I thought the music was good, but I wondered if Roy Orbison wouldn't be a hard sell in the teen market. It hadn't hurt Buddy Holly's career that he, like Roy, wore glasses, but Buddy Holly was better looking than Roy, who had a plump face with no jaw line to speak of. He was sort of on the pudgy side, plus he seemed to carry a gloomy air around with him. The only way he compared with Elvis was the pompadour.

Still, Jack had said he was a pretty good showman, despite seeming so introverted. Sam had got him the bookings through Bob Neal's agency, which Sam had some connection with or maybe a business interest in. When Roy was booked on shows with Carl Perkins and Johnny Cash, he had held his own because of his experience on radio and in the bands he had had ever since he was about fourteen years old.

Jerry Lee Lewis in Person

On a dark and gloomy Friday morning at the end of January 1958, the front door crashed open, a booted foot kicked in before the whole person could be seen, and lo, there appeared Mr. Jerry Lee Lewis in the flesh. I had anticipated this moment, and now I was finally getting to meet the singer I had been praising in print and conversation since last summer. I wasn't surprised by his swagger, that redneck stride that announced "better not get in my way," but I *was* unprepared to see how young he looked, and how tall. Maybe he looked shorter in pictures because he was usually seated at a piano. The famous mop of hair was quite noticeable, long only on top and wavy, and he had barely gotten inside the door when he whipped out a comb from his back pocket and ran it through the peroxided golden locks.

Perhaps "immature" is the better word, not "young," but I wouldn't have guessed we were about the same age. Maybe he seemed young because his father had come up with him from Ferriday, Louisiana. Elmo was even taller than Jerry Lee by a few inches, maybe six feet four, rail thin, with long arms that hung limply from stooped shoulders. His complexion was gray, and he wore a suspicious expression that made me shrink a little (maybe a hint of violence?). It was very clear that he was possessive and proud of his son and had come to defend him from whatever threats might exist at 706 Union. I had seen people like this walking the streets of South End in Corinth, but a person not from the South might say he looked like those photos of Okies on their trek to California during the Depression or Kentucky moonshiners the way the movies showed them to be.

Regina called Jack Clement to the front to greet the visitors. Jack and Jerry Lee got along well because it was Jack who had "discovered" him for Sun, and they probably wanted to talk about the session that was scheduled for the next day. Off they went to Taylor's café for some lunch.

Jerry's Session and a Visitor from the Big Apple

The next afternoon when I again saw Jerry Lee, he was in full character. The person I saw this time—singing and playing the piano—was not a kid but a man, a roiling, explosive package of energy and sound.

Normally, I didn't work on Saturday, but Sam had asked me to entertain Jerry Shifrin, a Roulette Records promotion man who was in town for the weekend. Jerry would doubtless have preferred to be with Sam, but Sam was hard to pin down. Shifrin had said on the phone he was headed our way on a sales tour through the South, but he might have been scouting talent in the way the Atlantic and Imperial guys, among others, had been doing for a long time.

I picked him up at his hotel in a rental car and showed him the Mississippi River Bridge, drove him through Overton Park and Zoo, and took him to lunch before facing the inevitable. I had to take him to the studio, which I knew would compare poorly with what I imagined to be a sophisticated Roulette studio in New York. Our one studio was about twenty by thirty-five feet, had five mikes, a few metal folding chairs, a piano, and the usual debris the musicians generated.

On the way to the studio, I told Jerry Shifrin the story of how Jerry Lee Lewis had first come to Sun in the fall of 1956. Sam was out of town, but Jerry insisted that somebody hear him. Sally buzzed Jack Clement in the control room and repeated to him what Jerry Lee had told her, that he played piano like Chet Atkins played the guitar. Jerry Lee sat down at the piano and proved it by playing "Wildwood Flower." That sounded pretty good to Jack, so he asked him what else he had. Billy Riley was there, too, with his bass tuned up to accompany the audition if need be. Jerry elected to do "Crazy Arms," and Jack rolled the tape.

When Sam returned and Jack played the tape for him, Sam exclaimed, "I can sell that." So "Crazy Arms," paired with "End of the Road," was duly issued, and it was only a year later that Jerry's big hit, "Whole Lot of Shakin' Going On," electrified the country. I told him the story of how I came to be with Sun, about answering Jerry Lee's fan mail, but now Kay Martin and Elaine Berman Orlando, who had formed the Jerry Lee Lewis fan club, had taken over that task.

When we arrived at the studio, we took the chance to walk to the control room during a break in taping and I introduced Jerry Shifrin to Jack Clement. Jack and the musicians went right ahead rehearsing numbers that were possible for the B-side of his next release. Since "Great Balls of Fire" was approaching a million in sales, they had again called on the noted songwriter Otis Blackwell for a follow-up for Jerry Lee, who didn't usually write his own material. They had been working on that number, "Breathless," before we arrived, Jack said, and it was coming along. Now they were considering several songs, including Roy Orbison's "Down the Line," which was eventually picked for the flip side. Sam would like the fact that Sun was to have in-house publishing for that one.

Jerry Lee was sitting at the piano bare-chested. It was wintertime, but the studio was fairly warm, and I guess he'd worked up a good sweat with his muscular piano playing. I had heard he gave it his all, whether for 10 people or 10,000, and the evidence was right before my eyes—this was a show! His pants were riding well below his waistline, exposing his "outie." The studio was smoky and littered with beer cans, and Jerry Lee was talking back and forth to Jack in the control room between takes or whenever Jack interrupted to start a new take.

I was standing behind Jack in the control room and Jerry Shifrin was at my side. I would have liked it to be a prettier scene, and I must have shaken my head just imagining what the visitor must think. I need not have worried, because Jerry Lee's playing and singing made up for his appearance. After we left, Jerry Shifrin told me how impressed he was with the sound we were hearing in the control room—the famous "Sun sound." As a person in sales, Jerry was more concerned with Sun's track record than an untidy studio or even Jerry's unkempt appearance. I knew the industry and the fans had great respect for the success of our label. I just wished we could have greater pride in our appearance.

End of an All-Day Date

Later Jerry Shifrin and I went to dinner at Justine's, a wonderful French restaurant in an old house in Memphis, eating artichokes and a tender, juicy steak with Béarnaise sauce. Afterwards we wound up at the Share-cropper, a semi-private club to which I had a key. Because of Memphis's strange liquor laws, mixed drinks couldn't be served by bars. But at a club such as this one, you could either bring a bottle with you for the bartender to use in making drinks, or you could even rent a locker, stock it, and have your booze at hand whenever you dropped by.

A singer with a sprinkle of gray in his hair was sitting at the piano accompanying himself. Mostly he played without singing, lost in his music. He seemed to be making love, not entertaining. He played dreamy standards like "Laura" and "Misty," and like so many lounge singers everywhere, was playing more for himself than for the people all around, who were so engrossed in their own conversations that they barely heard the music.

Sitting on one of the banquettes along the wall, I was one of those talking with just one ear out for the nice jazz-tinged music. I had a guest, and Jerry Shifrin and I talked an hour or more about the record business, the money to be made, and what kind of acts were selling now. Like me, he was single and fairly new to the business, still living at home with his parents. I gained some education that night in his account of why, in the record business, as in much of the entertainment industry, there was a preponderance of Jewish people. Some people I met in the business assumed or asked if I were Jewish.

Jerry introduced this subject and didn't seem reluctant to discuss what might have been a touchy subject. Of his own ethnic group, Jerry said that Jews liked to go where the money was because they desired protection and security. He said, "If you're called a 'dirty Jew bastard' enough times, and have your nose broken a few times, you learn that money is one way to keep yourself safe."

We left without knowing that the musician was Charlie Rich, later one of our artists at the record company. I got to know Charlie Rich in time, but Jerry Shifrin I never saw or heard from again, except for a lovely, prompt, and proper thank-you note he sent upon returning to New York.

Back home, reflecting on the evening's conversation, I recalled a comment Sam had made to me concerning wealth. "The only thing money can do for you is provide a measure of security." Sam had alluded to hardships in his family, telling how he delivered groceries as a young teen to help support his family during the Depression. As an adult, his drive to make money and hold onto it obviously derived from a fear of reliving those years of deprivation. But Sam also recognized another aspect of becoming prosperous, adding, "Once you have money, you are still yourself."

Me and Jerry Lee

There were repercussions to our visit to Jerry Lee's session, which went on for some time after we left. Sam had come in, and Jerry Lee was quick to corner him. He had said, "Mr. Phillips, you've got some bad women working for your company." Sam asked him what he meant and

Jerry said, "That Barnes woman. She came in here today and while I was recording, she was standing in the control room, just shaking her head."

"Now hold on, Jerry, you took it all wrong. She's a big fan of yours. She was shaking her head because she just couldn't believe any one person could have so much talent!" Sam reassured him. Jerry was satisfied with Sam's explanation.

Actually, I did like Jerry's singing and playing, despite my chagrin with his appearance that day. "Crazy Arms," "End of the Road," and especially "You Win Again," the B side of "Great Balls of Fire," were my favorites among his releases thus far. He captured so naturally that melancholy characteristic of the best country songs. "Whole Lot of Shakin'" and his other rock records appealed to me in varying degrees, but a few of his more suggestive touches were a little much. Later, as I wrote on the "Great Balls of Fire" EP notes, Jerry's lack of inhibition could at times be "almost embarrassing." Sam laughed when he read that phrase, but he understood my point that Jerry bordered on the obscene in some performances. Even Sam had doubts about the acceptability of "Whole Lot of Shakin'," fearing radio stations would find it too risqué to play. And it was less so than some of the later disks.

The leer in Jerry's delivery was coarser than the innuendoes or frank sexuality of the rhythm-and-blues music I had always liked. R&B was often clever and had sly irony in a way that Jerry's delivery did not. At a later Jerry Lee session, I hastened through the studio to get to the front during a break, and the girls asked me what was going on in the studio. I said, "Jerry Lee just had another orgasm." Whether I liked it or not, he was a trendsetter.

Ballad of a Teenage Queen

Jerry Lee's "Great Balls of Fire" had been riding high on all the charts and staying at #1 on the country charts for weeks. On February 3, 1958, another Sun hit took its place as #1, "Ballad of a Teenage Queen," sung by Johnny Cash and composed by our A&R man, Jack Clement.

Jack was musically versatile, having played in country, Hawaiian, and polka bands in Boston, Washington, and elsewhere on the East Coast and around the Memphis area for several years. He played a variety of instruments, and listened to all types of music. One day I opened the control room door to be greeted by the strains of classical guitar, probably Segovia. To tweak him, I exclaimed, "Jack, you've been practicing!"

But country was his love. He said when he was a little boy and didn't have a good radio, he would put a coat hanger on his big toe and prop his leg up on the bed to get better reception for the Grand Ole Opry. He liked the old-fashioned sound of Kentucky bluegrass, as well as traditional ballads. The tunes he wrote showed all these influences at times.

Johnny Cash had recorded "Ballad of a Teenage Queen" late in 1957 and was pushing it on his many appearances, live and on TV and radio. I hadn't seen this star yet, because of his constant bookings, which were so lucrative that he had given up a regular spot on the Grand Ole Opry.

Sam had initially been the one to record Johnny, producing his two previous hits, "Folsom Prison Blues" and "I Walk the Line," and most of those on the album for which I'd written the liner notes. He had gradually been turning over the studio work to Jack and Bill Justis, and Jack was Johnny Cash's producer.

Jack was not inclined to continue in Sam's R&B groove, instead looking toward Nashville for inspiration. In a nod to the Anita Kerr Singers of RCA, Jack brought in the Gene Lowery Singers to back Johnny Cash on "Ballad of a Teenage Queen." In the title and story of young romance, he made an appeal to the teenage record-buying public. This record did not have the stark quality of Cash's earlier releases, and the softer sound was largely responsible for the record's making it to the top twenty of the pop charts for the first time. Clearly, Cash was picking up that target audience of teenagers with this record, while still maintaining his popularity with the country fans.

I felt pretty sure they were buying it for the B side, "Big River," a Cash composition which was a much more arresting record to me. Somewhat folk-sounding with Jack Clement's nice acoustic guitar playing, it had an insistent rhythm that flowed through the story of a man chasing an elusive woman all the way down the Mississippi River from St. Paul, Minnesota, to New Orleans. Humor shines through on some of Cash's rhymes in the tune, as in "cavorting in Davenport." The title "Big River" had been suggested by Carl Perkins, who thereby repaid the debt he owed Johnny for suggesting the title of his smash hit, "Blue Suede Shoes." (Carl also came up with the title of "I Walk the Line.")

His loyal country audience made the record #1 on the country chart, a first for Cash. This development was not surprising, given that in 1957 he had been the third-selling country artist in the country, just behind Marty Robbins and Ray Price. Some of the long-time listeners evidently didn't like Cash's characteristic sound to be tampered with, and one went so far as to write me complaining of the Gene Lowery Singers.

First Trip to New York

My daily talks with Jud continued to be a saga of his adventures, not all connected with selling records. One day he reported meeting Christine Jorgensen at a party. She was the first person the public knew of being transformed from a man into a woman through surgical, hormonal, and other mysterious means. Late-night TV host Jack Paar was having a field day at her expense, but Jud said when he met her at a party she was pleasant and "right attractive."

Another time he told of being propositioned by a reputed Mafia man in Buffalo who offered Jud $1,000 to sleep with his wife. She'd been looking him over in a restaurant, and Jud said it took all his diplomacy to convey to this man that his wife was certainly a desirable woman but that he just had to say "no" to this suggestion in respect for the marital vows of himself and the lady.

Jud spent more time in New York than anywhere else. On February 15 he was there to witness the kickoff of the Dick Clark Saturday night "Beechnut Show." Clark's afternoon "American Bandstand" was popular, and now he was making the big leap. Jud had placed several of our artists on the weekday show and had developed a good relationship with Tony Mammarella, Dick Clark's producer, and other staff.

Jerry Lee was one of the featured performers on this premiere, along with Pat Boone, Connie Francis, Johnnie Ray, and Chuck Willis. Jerry Lee was doing his monster hit, "Great Balls of Fire," as well as his brand-new release, "Breathless." Jerry Lee was the hottest act on the show, having sold a million copies of "Great Balls of Fire" in December and reaching #2 on the pop charts, #3 in R&B, #1 in country, and #1 in the United Kingdom charts. The single would stay on the charts for a total of twenty-one weeks—what the trade papers termed "a smash."

Jerry Lee caused a lot of excitement on the show, and all was well in New York, according to Jud, who called me the next week saying it was time for me to come there to get to know some people in the trade. "You need to be able to meet these people and talk to them. Then when you call them, they'll know who they're talking to. I'm going to call Sam at home just as soon as I get off the phone."

Almost immediately Sam called. "Jud wants you to come to New York, and I guess it would be a good idea. I'm getting Sally to book you on American for tomorrow evening. Jud will get you a room at the Manhattan."

New York had been like a mirage to me all my life—radio programs coming from there, movies filmed there, Holden Caulfield wandering around there in *The Catcher in the Rye.* Sometime in the past year I had even day-dreamed about going there. Now it was going to happen! But all I could think of was getting my beige cashmere coat cleaned and my other clothes assembled so I could look my best on the trip.

I borrowed Bill Justis's car and rushed home to get my coat and drop it off at Nunnery's Cleaners. The next day I was able to don it along with my black traveling suit, three-inch black heels, a little black hat with a veil, and three-quarter-length gloves that came to just the point where I pushed up the sleeves of the spiffy, freshly cleaned coat. The plane left just at dusk and stopped in Washington. While we were on the ground I lit a cigarette. I had flown so little I didn't know that was forbidden. A very agitated steward leapt toward me and commanded me to "put out that cigarette before you blow up the airplane."

It seemed we were barely airborne from Washington when we were circling into LaGuardia over the East River, the wing on my side dipping toward the dark water and a million lights on either bank. It was an unforgettable sight: geometric shapes outlined in brilliant starpoints jutting into the black canopy.

A taxi hurled me to Times Square and the Manhattan Hotel, where Jud was waiting to check me in and order me a bourbon and water in the bar. It was real! I was in New York on business! Jud and I were a promotion team. People in the bar treated us like old friends, and it was comfortable and easy.

A Country Girl in the City

But my hotel troubles began as soon as I went up to bed. The radiator was putting out suffocating steam; the furniture seemed to be crowding in on me and bumping me when I moved around; the window wouldn't open to give me a breath of fresh air. When I lay down to sleep, the sirens shrieked and screamed continuously. Hammering and buzzing from a construction project in the hotel went on all night.

I walked out of the hotel about 2:00 a.m. to breathe some cool air but hastily came back in when a man began following me. The Hispanic elevator operator didn't speak English, it seemed, because he took me up past my floor and I had to ride down with him alone. It was scary.

I slept very little and was groggy when awakened at eight o'clock by a knock from room service. I went to the door to find a bellman with a bouquet of exquisite red roses. I handed them back to him, saying, "They're not for me, I don't know anyone here." But he asked my name and compared it to the card, and amazingly they were for me. The card read, "Welcome to New York. Grelun Landon, Hill and Range Songs." Aside from the orchids my boyfriends had sent me for dances in college, no one had ever sent me flowers. I found getting roses first thing in the morning very acceptable, just like in the movies.

I turned on the radio and heard WCBS reporting the eight o'clock news. It struck me—they're telling the local news, and it's the news of the world. I am at the center of the known universe!

Meeting Exciting People

I had to calm down and get ready for breakfast with Grelun Landon, and heaven knows I dreaded that. Hill and Range Songs—songs I knew so little about. How could I make conversation and appear professional? I knew that the company had bought one of Sam Phillips's publishing companies, Hi Lo Music, in 1955 and had thereby gained exclusive rights to Elvis's songs. Also, Elvis's manager, Col. Tom Parker, had an agreement with Hill and Range concerning their involvement in picking future tunes from their catalog for Elvis to record. The company had an ongoing relationship with Sam and Sun, publishing the sheet music for all his publishing companies and perhaps performing other services that I didn't know about.

It was a great relief when the friendly and urbane Mr. Landon, after the usual inquiries about my trip and such, began to tell me about his bosses, brothers Julian and Jean Aberbach. They were Austrian immigrants who had found great success publishing country music, but a secondary passion of theirs was collecting modern art. From Art History 302 at the University of Alabama, I knew a bit about Modigliani, Kandinsky, and others, so when he told me that these were the artists the Aberbachs displayed in their offices, I was able to be sincerely impressed and even pronounce the artists' names.

This part of the day had gotten off to a good start. Then it was time to meet Jud and go to *Billboard*, the most prestigious magazine in the music business, with offices upstairs over the Palace Theater. There I met legendary music editor Paul Ackerman, one of the first in the industry to appreciate the importance of our music and someone Sam liked and admired greatly.

One of the editorial staff asked if I'd ever before seen snow. I laid on the southern accent and exclaimed what a surprise it was to see that gray, slushy stuff all over the curbs. I thought, "Yankees do love their fixed ideas about the South, so why disillusion them?" I'd known snowsuits, snow boots, and snowmen all my life, but I couldn't tell them that.

Another stop was at *Cashbox*, another trade publication, where I met Marty Ostrow. I was learning to put the names with the faces I had seen on the mastheads and the voices on the telephone.

Dick Clark, Chuck Berry, and Johnny Carson—All in One Night

Saturday night, February 22, 1958, brought an event to remember. Jud had arranged for tickets for the dress rehearsal for the Dick Clark show at the Little Theatre on West Forty-fourth Street at Broadway. We had access to the production floor, and it was a thrill to me, the radio-TV college major, to see how the cameras and the set were arranged and how the crew was working. Unlike his weekday show from Philadelphia, this thirty-minute production had no dancing. We sat with the rest of the audience in theater seats, and I didn't meet Dick Clark or any of the guests.

Chuck Berry's "Sweet Little Sixteen" stole the show for me. Though I was past the age of identifying with his clever lyrics of teenage love, car races, and school hassles, I found this performer a sight to behold. He was very dark, with pleasant chiseled features, and a body as flexible as a sapling. His little duck-walk across the entire stage was humorous.

He was similar to Elvis and the other current rock 'n' rollers in that he played the guitar, sang to and for teenagers, and produced hits one after the other, yet he wasn't reviled by the puritanical critics the way Elvis and the other white players were. There wasn't as much to criticize, maybe. In contrast to Jerry Lee, he didn't deal much in suggestive lyrics, and he had shaken off the lowdown images of the R&B that went before rock 'n' roll. You could understand his lyrics—some said Elvis and others mumbled—and they sounded more playful than sexy. Finally, he *was* black, not a white man sounding black. A convoluted prejudice made it worse for a white man to sound black.

Still, Chuck Berry was a bridge between black and white cultures, for he had cultivated a big white following in his native St. Louis, just as Fats Domino had done in New Orleans. At one time Berry had played R&B and country music, but now he was strictly writing songs for teens to dance to.

Dick Clark interviewed all his guests, including a rising ABC-TV performer, Johnny Carson, and the president of Jerry Lee's fan club, Elaine Berman. But the music was of course the main attraction, even though it was lip-synced.

After the broadcast, Jud and I went out with a couple of young women from the ABC network. We had drinks with them and with Bill Justis, who had also come up to appear on the show. His tunes "Raunchy" and "College Man" were featured, and Bill had looked cute in his little college beanie. Before "College Man," he had worn a toupee, or as he called it, a "rug," to cover his bald pate. He was flying back to Memphis early the next day, and when he said he had to leave, the party broke up. I concluded he was getting back to his wife, Yvonne, and his work on the brick barbeque pit and fence he was building in his backyard. As he put it, he was "queer for bricks," and brick masonry was his safety valve for the pressures of suddenly being a recording star.

Sampling Café Society

Jud asked if there were any place else I'd like to go. The New Yorker had mentioned that Mabel Mercer was playing at RSVP, a supper club on East Fifty-fifth. Jud hailed a taxi, and off we went uptown to this tiny place. It was much more intimate than the image I had built up in my mind from its legend as a premier watering hole of New York café society.

Mabel was sitting in a spotlight on a little stage not far from our table. Backed by her piano player, she half-sang, half-talked selections from the greats like Cole Porter and George Gershwin. When her break came, she headed for Jud and they embraced like old friends. He invited her to sit and have something to drink, which she did. They didn't explain how they knew each other, but Jud seemed to have dreams of becoming her manager.

Jud launched into a mesmerizing scene, envisioning Mabel as a TV star. He would arrange her setting and flowing gown just so, with lighting to dramatize her power and high seriousness. She was hanging onto every word, as he created this great drama. He told her she would be another Marian Anderson, known to everyone, enumerating spirituals she could sing. I was agape that this rock 'n' roll promoter was friends with Mabel Mercer. From what I read she was from a world apart from that of Jud and me—the darling of the sophisticates in New York, France, and the Caribbean. Neither Jud nor Mabel hinted at any context for this encounter.

During her next set, Mabel's protégé, Bobby Short, joined us during his break from the gig he was playing across the street at the Blue Angel. I must admit I found more glamour in these two celebrated cabaret singers than in the fellows I was promoting at Sun. The four of us chatted as if we saw each other every day, and then they went back to work and Jud and I set off for a downtown diner. Jud was wound up, talking about our artists and our company. It was well after two when we finally said goodnight at the Manhattan.

A Notorious Clergyman and a Decadent Lunch

When Sunday came, Jud had fixed me up with Harry Apostoleris, a bachelor whom I had met when we paid a visit to his distributorship in New York, Alpha Records. Harry asked if he could show me around New York on Sunday, and what did I want to see? I told him I wanted to go to services at St. John the Divine Cathedral.

Early Sunday morning he picked me up in his luxurious black Lincoln, driving through trash-strewn streets where the store fronts had metal grilles, almost to Harlem on the Upper East Side, finding the unfinished cathedral wrapped in scaffolding. Inside, it was likewise a work in progress.

I had wanted to hear the Dean of St. John the Divine, the Very Reverend James Pike, because he was the Episcopal Church's most controversial clergyman. I admired him for the outspoken way he confronted issues involving social justice. He was loved or hated because of his activism in civil rights, women's roles in the church, and other causes that were radical in the '50s.

His sermon admonished the hearers to behold the neighborhood surrounding the church, to serve and not ignore or reject the poor. When it came time for communion, I encountered half a dozen black clergy serving at the altar. Harry asked me later how it felt to receive communion from black hands. It felt good, I told him. In this soaring space, with heavenly music and the prophetic voice of Dr. Pike, it was indeed, as the Prayer Book would say, "meet and right so to do." Harry said the service was like the Greek Orthodox church of his upbringing, adding that, when the astronauts went up into orbit, they didn't see God there, which settled the question of God's existence for Harry.

When my host asked me to suggest a restaurant for lunch, I hesitated but when urged I ventured, "The Russian Tea Room?" Harry vetoed that idea, stating, "It's a factory," stressing the "ac" in that New York way. Instead, he drove us to Le Chambord, where the maitre d' greeted Harry expansively and seated us in a banquette along the wall where I could see fashionably dressed people being served food that looked and smelled divine.

Every time Harry would ask if I would have something, I would say "yes": cocktail, escargot, Dover sole, salade, vin blanc, tarte, café. Lunch lasted a very long time, and it was the very best meal of my life. Better even than the New Orleans restaurants where I'd learned how good cuisine could be: Brennan's, Commander's Palace, Broussard's, Galatoire's, Arnaud's, and Antoine's. It was gourmet heaven. I read later in Herb Caen's San Francisco *Chronicle* column that Le Chambord was at that time New York's finest, and the world's most expensive, restaurant: $6.50 for a cup of soup the least costly item. I hadn't known, because Harry ordered for me.

The next morning Jud rang me up to tell me what time we needed to leave for the airport. I was flying back to Memphis alone, but he was going to take me to the plane. We met in the coffee shop, and Jud was bursting with the news that he had just talked to Sam.

"I got my brother on the phone while I was waiting for you—woke him up. He just about fell out of bed when I told him you had taken Harry Apostoleris to church! Church! You took Harry Apostoleris to church! Sam couldn't believe it." Jud was chuckling and shaking his head, but I failed to see why going to church should be so humorous.

"Then I told him what you had for lunch. You want to know what Sam said?"

"He said, 'That son-of-a-bitch Harry Apostoleris has done everything a distributor can think of to do to a manufacturer, but he ain't never fed me *snails!*'" At this Jud roared, and the bored New York waitress filled our coffee cups with a look on her face that said, "Well, it takes all kinds."

We got to the airport late and had to run for the American plane that was literally waiting for *me* on the runway. As we dashed past counter after counter Jud would nod or smile at the people standing at their posts and they would all say, "Hello, Mr. Phillips. Hello, Mr. Phillips. Hello, Mr. Phillips." He was a member of the Million Mile Club, and I swear this is what happened, bizarre as it sounds. Everyone in New York at American Airlines knew Jud, and once he had delivered me up the steps of the big red, white, and blue DC-7, a stewardess personally settled me in my seat and then the plane could take off.

When I got home I couldn't wait to tell my landlady all that had happened in New York, including meeting Mabel Mercer and Bobby Short. What did she say? She said, "So you were sitting there, at that table, with two *niggers*?" I was speechless, but my heart had been stabbed.

"College Man" Follows "Raunchy"

Even though Bill Justis had performed "College Man" on the Dick Clark show, we hadn't shipped it yet, and I asked Bill about this when we next met in the Sun office. He said, "Sam is holding off so it won't interfere with the sales of 'Raunchy.' It's not a good idea to have two singles out at the same time."

But soon after our trip to New York, the follow-up record was sent to our sampling list and the orders started pouring in. Even so, "Raunchy" remained the hit, staying on the charts for twenty-six weeks, and went far beyond the million-seller it had been in 1957. But the phenomenal thing was, two other artists also made the charts with their cover records of "Raunchy." Lew Chudd of Imperial on the West Coast put it out with Ernie Freeman, and it stayed on the charts, especially the R&B charts where Imperial was so strong, for several weeks. Randy Wood's Dot cover with the Billy Vaughn Orchestra was even more successful.

During one of our daily phone conversations, Jud had told me about the flip side of Billy Vaughn's single. It was a sentimental ballad, "Sail Along Silvery Moon," and when he heard it and subsequently ran into Randy Wood on his travels, Jud said, "Man, you are pushing the wrong side of that record." Randy Wood took Jud's advice and laid into "Sail Along," with the result that it went to #5 on the *Billboard* pop chart and became one of the biggest sellers Dot had that year. In addition, Vaughn's "Raunchy" also made the charts for a double-sided hit. "College Man" sold a respectable number of records, but never made it into the top ten.

Since he thought of himself as an arranger and bandleader rather than an artist, I asked Bill how it felt to have had such great success the first time out of the gate. "A gas, man! Never would have thought it," he said, adding that he felt he owed Jud much gratitude for all he'd done to make the record a success. "I bought him a suit of clothes, man, to thank him," Bill said, adding that this was an insignificant gesture in relation to all he had gained. Sam also was due credit in having the imagination to introduce the first rock 'n' roll instrumental, which was soon being imitated by a variety of guitar players.

"I hear you putting down a lot of what's being played around this place, but I have the feeling you really liked 'Raunchy,'" I commented to Bill.

"I did like that tune. Sid Manker (the guitarist in Bill's band) wrote it, you know. Based it on a folk melody. We had been playing it for dances, and the audiences seemed to really dig it. It was just a fluke that I played that funky saxophone solo, though. I had hired a real sax man for the session, but he didn't show, so I was drafted. Some bad sax playing, man."

Now We're Selling Chewing Gum

About the time Kay was working as fast as possible mailing "College Man" to a long list of trade publications, distributors, and radio stations, Jud called with his latest scheme. He had run it by Sam, who reluctantly agreed, but it involved a lot of work.

It seemed Beechnut Gum wasn't getting the response they'd hoped for sponsoring "American Bandstand." The Dick Clark people had confided this information to Jud, who came up with a scheme to promote Beechnut Gum and Jerry Lee Lewis's next Sun release, "Breathless," at the same time. Jud met with Clark's ad agency, Young and Rubicam, to plan a campaign whereby each person who sent in five Beechnut wrappers and fifty cents would receive an autographed (stamped, that is) copy of Jerry's record. The dual promotion of Beechnut and "Breathless" on

Dick Clark's national TV show was doubtless a reason it climbed to #7 on the *Billboard* pop chart, #3 on R&B, and #4 on country, despite not being too easy to dance to.

The catch was that we had to process all the requests, pack the records, and ship them. Young and Rubicam had sent a representative to visit the Sun facilities and see how we could rearrange our storage room so that all of us on the staff, plus any musicians we could draft, and some temporary help could do all that processing. Somehow, we managed to ship 48,000 records.

I was surprised at the number of overall sales, in addition to the promotional sales, because the record was not nearly as strong as "Whole Lot of Shakin'" or "Great Balls of Fire." But Jud was happy, Dick Clark was happy, and a lot of teenagers were happy. This third hit was good for Jerry Lee's personal appearances, helping him get a booking with the Alan Freed rock 'n' roll all-stars tour from March until May. After that, a big British tour was booked. So everybody was happy except Sam, who didn't like anything about the promotion because he had to foot the bill for the extra labor to do all that shipping.

Sam was a close man with the dollar. When I had rented the car to drive around the Roulette man, Jerry Shifrin, a question had been raised about the mileage the bill registered. I told Sally I hadn't driven as far as their charges reflected, and I called the rental company and got the billing changed because it indeed was their mistake. After my New York trip, Sam dropped a hint about the hotel's charges for "valet service," which indeed I had incurred to have a couple of dresses pressed. I had wanted to make a good impression and didn't think the charges were out of line, but apparently Sam watched every penny that went out and woe to the one who wasted his money.

The Man in the Blue Suede Shoes

One morning in early March, a lanky fellow came in the door and asked if Mr. Phillips could see him. Regina politely told him Sam wasn't in, but the visitor said he would wait in the studio. He seemed to know his way around and proceeded to go through the door to the studio, where he sat for several hours in a metal folding chair. He never came out to go for coffee or lunch or to speak with us.

When I walked to the front of the building and then returned to the back, I glanced at him but never did say more than "hi." At first I just saw a man with curly hair, a receding hairline, and an air of profound dejection. He was so thin as to look malnourished. A more experienced person would have known it was a look connected with alcoholism, but I didn't recognize that. Something about his sadness and humility reminded me of those stray dogs that would come around our farmhouse looking for scraps.

Then it dawned on me. I've seen that man's picture—it's Carl Perkins! Still I didn't introduce myself, partly because he seemed so detached. Also, I had taken the attitude that I was there to do my work, and if the musicians didn't initiate talk with me, I usually didn't talk much with them. The regulars like Billy Riley, Stan Kesler, and Roland Janes were exceptions.

When Sam came in about two o'clock, I was in the front and was the one to tell him Carl Perkins had been in the studio waiting for him a long time. Sam's expression didn't change, but his voice said a lot. "Carl Perkins" was all he said. But the irony in those two words conveyed a great deal of negativity. They got together for awhile and then Carl left. He probably had come to ask about having another session, but he must've gotten a rejection, because he never showed up again to my knowledge.

Carl's album was selling pretty well, and I looked for a chance to ask Sam why we weren't promoting Carl more. Jud had booked him for the Dick Clark nighttime show that summer, so he wasn't totally forgotten, but we didn't have a current record. When I asked him about this, he told me that he had pinned a lot of hope on Carl after he sold Elvis, and it looked like his hopes were being realized with the success of Carl's million-seller, "Blue Suede Shoes." Sam had bought Carl a nice toupee and the requisite Cadillac in celebration.

"He came to me after hearing 'Blue Moon of Kentucky' by Elvis Presley on Bob Neal's radio show from Memphis. Carl was at home in

Jackson, playing around there with his two brothers, and he said he did the same type of music Elvis was doing. When he came here, he brought a drummer, too, and some songs he had written. I've been working with him for three years, but he's never had a commercial record except 'Blue Suede Shoes.'"

"But that was really big," I replied. "And I loved it."

"Yes, if he hadn't missed his timing, the momentum of that record could have been a springboard to bigger things. It wasn't his fault his driver went to sleep and had a wreck on the way to New York for his big TV appearance, but by the time he and his brothers were out of the hospital and could work again, Elvis's cover had come out and the public was confused. Instead of Carl singing the song on the Perry Como show as he had been booked to do, Elvis did it on the Ed Sullivan show."

"We have Steve Sholes and RCA to thank for that," Sam added sarcastically.

He went on to say that he had had a session on Carl just the past December, and had put out "Glad All Over," but it wasn't going anywhere. "You haven't noticed any big stir, have you?"

"You know, Sam, I remember vaguely reading about Carl and Elvis getting together at this studio but not to record—just goofing around. That was before I knew much about Sun Records. Was that when you were still trying to get a good release for him?"

"Oh, yessss—," he drawled. "Carl was having a session, and what you might call a major disruption took place. Elvis came in and took over. He sat down at the piano and started singing gospel, and all the cats joined in. Jerry Lee was playing piano for Carl—first time Carl had had a piano for a session and the first time Jerry Lee had played on one. I called up Johnny Cash to come over, and also Robert Johnson, the entertainment editor from the paper, and Leo Soroka—you know them. They took some pictures and the next day the *Press-Scimitar* carried a photo of the guys, calling them 'The Million Dollar Quartet.' That was December 1956, after Elvis had left us. But he still had the habit of coming by.

"But back to Carl. I don't know we can get any more out of him than we already have. He's a good country singer, but that's not necessarily an asset in today's market. That's not the way we're going now. Country is just the same as dead. If you don't believe it, ask anybody in Nashville."

Chicago Skyline

In April I made my next big-city excursion with Jud, this time to the convention of the Music Operators of America. This was the organization that represented jukeboxes and other coin-operated entertainment devices. My introduction to Chicago began with that anthill of an airline terminal, O'Hare Field. Jud had instructed me to take a taxi to the Morrison Hotel, which appeared very tall and grandiose, also teeming with people as I arrived.

This trip turned out to be entirely different from the one to New York, where we were on the go every minute, meeting our contacts. Here Jud stationed himself in the bar and let the DJs, distributors, and fellow manufacturers come to him. A couple of women of no particular function in the record industry came by, too. I didn't try to match him drink for drink and played a very passive role as he entertained his many acquaintances with his never-ending gab. Some of the labels had scheduled meetings with their distributors, but Sun hadn't done that, and we didn't have a hospitality suite. Jud said Roulette had a big reception room with a roulette wheel in it, and other shenanigans were said to be going on. Roulette's owner, Morris Levy, was a reputed mobster who owned the nightclub Birdland.

The meetings were geared to the business matters concerning people who owned and operated jukeboxes and other coin machines, so many of the concerns they brought up were only indirectly relevant to our business and we didn't attend. Sun didn't sell directly to jukebox operators, though we did do business with a few so-called "one-stops" that carried a variety of lines where jukebox operators could select new records for their machines.

I read in Billboard later that one of the topics discussed in the meetings was public relations. "Many public officials have a bad opinion of the music-machine industry," one speaker was quoted as saying, adding that the members should get to know their local law enforcement officials, as well as important politicians. The Kefauver Commission, headed by our Tennessee Senator Estes Kefauver, early in the 1950s had reported that the coin-machine industry was largely dominated by the underworld in the big cities of the East and Great Lakes regions, so "bad opinion" was indeed an understatement. Before I left Memphis to go to the convention, Bill Justis had told me to beware in Chicago, quipping that, when these guys met, each one brought "two big bottles, two blonds, and two bodyguards."

The operators were also worried that 1958 would be a lean year because of the recession the U.S. economy had fallen into. Our sales had been good so far, but Jud reported that some of the other manufacturers said business was soft. The trend would catch up with us before long.

The MOA organization also discussed the fear that the American Society of Composers, Authors, and Publishers (ASCAP) was going to levy taxes on each jukebox play. They asserted that the organization was so rich and powerful that they could hire lawyers who would silence any MOA objections to their proposed assessments.

I had known of ASCAP through my college broadcasting courses and because I became friends with an ASCAP auditor, Marvin Brown, who was going through the logs of KALB radio when I worked at their TV affiliate in Alexandria, Louisiana. ASCAP collected royalties for the publishers and composers each time one of their licensed songs was played live or in broadcasts. Having ASCAP collect jukebox royalties was a threat to the profits of all jukebox owners, but it was rumored that the biggest concern was that underworld operators would lose their system of using cash receipts to launder money that could then be used for illegal activities.

Sun had no connection with ASCAP because we went through Broadcast Music, Inc. (BMI). This group had been formed because ASCAP, as a traditional Tin Pan Alley licensing agency, was reluctant to admit the hillbilly, blues, and R&B music publishers. Sun had several publishing subsidiaries through BMI that brought in consistent royalties.

The exhibits featured the most innovative sound equipment, and in 1958, everything was about stereo. The technology had just been introduced for records to be pressed in this multi-track format. This development caused consternation among the jukebox owners, who were facing a switch from monophonic to stereo that might be costly. They didn't discuss how the newly marketed transistor radios would cut into their business, but they should have been worried about that, too.

I was still learning about the record business, and this meeting was another important chapter in my education. Just listening to Jud, whether he was talking to others or to me directly, was not only entertaining but informative about how the vast network involved in producing and disseminating recorded music actually worked.

It was fascinating, but I had to go to my room a couple of hours each day to take care of some Sun business that was going on as usual between Memphis and our far-flung associates. I tried to pull Jud away from the bar a few times, saying we needed to go make some phone calls, but my entreaties fell on deaf ears. So I would leave him in the bar sitting, talking, and drinking.

You'd think Jud would get tired or drunk, but when we met to go to dinner each evening, Jud was as fresh and alert as if it were morning. The first night we went to the new Polynesian restaurant, Trader Vic's, which had recently opened in the Palmer House. The experience of drinking a Mai Tai with a little straw in it, eating tidbits toasted on a skewer, and sinking into the tropical atmosphere of leafy plants and trickling water was altogether pleasant.

The second night, two old friends from the days I worked at KALB in Alexandria, Dick and Jackie Chaussee, met us at the Pump Room of the Ambassador East Hotel. This was Chicago's most exclusive restaurant, the one you would see photographed when movie stars, national politicians, or international celebrities visited Chicago. As we eased into the comfortable seating in that quietly elegant landmark, I was thinking, "This wouldn't be hard to get used to." The food was good, and the service was beautifully refined. Jud charmed the Chaussees, taking from his wallet pictures of his wife, Dean, and son, Juddy, to show my friends, thus implying and assuring them that he wasn't leading their friend down a path of sin. We could have gone to the banquet instead and heard

Connie Francis sing, but dinner in this posh dining room was so much nicer.

I stayed only two days and thus didn't get to look in on the very last event of the convention, which was listed as a Ladies Hospitality Suite open house at 7:00 p.m. This was a nod to members who had brought their wives. It was assumed that there were not any ladies working in this industry. Jud stayed behind to visit radio and TV stations in the Chicago area while I flew back to Memphis, flush with the excitement of being in the midst of some big players in a big industry.

Johnny Cash, the Tennessee Two, and Jack Clement

Jack Clement and I were getting to be buddies, and I especially enjoyed those times we would sit in the studio together and he would sing and play the guitar just for me. He had written a great many songs, and he was gradually introducing me to most of them. The one I liked best was "The Best Guitar Picker in Shelby County," which had the lines "I would sit there by the hour / Picking Wildwood Flower," describing how he labored to achieve his goal of proficiency and recognition as a guitar player.

One particular day, Jack stuck his head in my office and said, "B.B., come out here. I have a new song I want you to hear."

I liked it. It was not a novelty like so many of Jack's songs, nor a ballad. It was sort of a weeper, "Guess Things Happen That Way," but philosophical not maudlin. Jack had written this lament about love gone wrong for Johnny Cash.

"When is he coming in?" I asked Jack.

"This week. That's why I wrote it." If Cash liked it, if Jack got a good cut, and if Sam agreed, this would be a nice follow-up for "Teenage Queen."

I was excited, because I had been preoccupied with this person, Johnny Cash, and his music since last summer—writing about him, touting his records—and yet I'd never seen him. It was early April of 1958 when he finally drove up in a 1956 Lincoln. He had cut "Ballad of a Teenage Queen" the previous December, and even though it was still charting in the trades, it was time for a follow-up.

John had been touring almost constantly in the United States and Canada, responding to the ever-growing demand for his act on live shows. His charisma and ability to relate to the audience were growing as he gained confidence, and his increased following was resulting in great record sales for us. Teenagers flocked to his shows, despite the serious demeanor that made him seem older than he actually was. Parents didn't hate him, because unlike Elvis and some others, Johnny wasn't considered a moral threat, his beat was not inflammatory, and his concerts didn't turn into pandemonium.

Soon after Johnny arrived for the session, he was joined by the Tennessee Two, his backing band. Marshall Grant was his slightly chubby bass player, and the taller, rail-thin Luther Perkins was his lead guitarist. Something about Luther was amusing, just to look at him, and he was often the butt of jokes both in the studio and on stage. According to Jack, Luther always played just the same—never any better and never any worse—with limited musical facility and a total lack of confidence. When he got nervous in a session, he would mess up at a critical time, and sometimes they had to do take after take. Yet, he was an essential part of the Cash sound, with his individualistic guitar licks. Marshall Grant had remarked that he and Luther were so bad they were good. Cash teased that he hired them in the early days because they were auto mechanics and could keep his old Dodge running while going from one show to the next. Jimmy Wilson deigned to come down from his den over Mrs. Taylor's restaurant to play piano, and J. M. Van Eaton rounded out the band for this session.

I paused in the control room off and on throughout the session, as they cut Jack's tune, "Guess Things Happen That Way." I could tell it was not going to have the thump-thump country sound that Sam had produced—it was more lyrical and pop sounding. The proposed B side was a little more typical of the Cash sound, "Come In Stranger." John said he had written this one on the road, thinking of what his wife Vivian always said to greet him when he made it home. The session lasted several hours, with the musicians trying out various tunes. Among a bunch of false starts, they ended up with what Jack thought would be at least two good possibilities for the next release and maybe a couple more.

When he arrived in late afternoon that day, Sam pronounced "Guess Things Happen That Way" a hit. "That's a stone, man, a rolling stone," he exclaimed. "This damn record is flat commercial. That line 'I don't like it / But I guess things happen that way' sticks in your brain." Jack was relieved, because Sam hadn't liked "Ballad of a Teenage Queen" and had been reluctant to release it. Sam also liked "Come In Stranger," so we had our next release. Sam's prediction was accurate, because "Guess Things Happen That Way" stayed on the charts twenty-four weeks, including eight weeks at #1. In my publicity for the record, I termed it a two-sided hit because "Come In Stranger" was having a good run on the country charts, climbing to #6 in the nation.

In view of this success, we were happy we'd invested a bit in a very nice sleeve with a pensive-looking Johnny Cash, all in black, sitting on a stool and smoking a cigarette. The photograph and sleeve design had the stark quality that was so often present in Johnny's work. This would be his fourth #1 record, and I pointed out in the notes on the back of the sleeve that "the DJs, juke box operators, and music fans who picked Johnny Cash the most promising new country artist of 1956 have not been disappointed in their choice."

Concerning the remainder of the session, Sam didn't find anything else to be enthusiastic about. John had recorded "Oh, Lonesome Me," but Sam didn't think he'd put it out because Don Gibson already had a hit on that number. I liked it so much, however, that I asked Jack to make me an acetate to take home, which he did a day or two later. He knew we'd both be in big trouble if anyone found out. He warned me, "This is just for you to listen to." He stressed the "you" and also "listen."

A Case of Musical Borrowing

During the lunch break during the day of the session, practically the whole staff and musicians descended upon Taylor's Restaurant. I ended up at a booth alone with Johnny Cash. My intention was to compliment him when I said, "I think it was great what you did with that Gordon Jenkins number."

He knew at once that I was referring to his adaptation of "Folsom

Prison Blues." Borrowings and mutations were common in traditional music, so my question was not meant to be an accusation. Still, he sputtered and became very defensive, saying, "I told Sam about that."

I happened to know "Crescent City Blues," the prototype of "Folsom Prison Blues," because my friend Jack Christian had sent me the relatively obscure LP, "Seven Dreams," a song sequence by Gordon Jenkins with a narrative line involving a train ride across the country and its stop in a small town where a young woman felt trapped. When I heard "Folsom Prison Blues," I realized he had used the same melody and made only minor changes in the lyrics. The rub was that this song was copyrighted, not one of those traditional ballads that attract variations.

I wondered if Sam realized that listing Cash as writer of "Folsom Prison" was exposing him to another suit like the one by Don Robey concerning "Bear Cat," but I didn't say anything. Publishing had nothing to do with my job. But I liked the Cash version, just thought it would have been better if somehow the origins had been given credit.

My introducing this subject caused uneasiness in our conversation, practically ended it that day, and I regretted that I had missed this chance to get to know Johnny Cash better.

Disturbing Development with Johnny Cash

The success of "Guess Things Happen That Way" had been generated by many factors. *Billboard* and *Cashbox* had carried great reviews, I had stayed on the phone constantly just after release with our distributors, who were ordering and re-ordering like mad. Jud was able to line up some more national TV guest spots for Johnny. Jack Clement contributed to giving Cash his first big "middle of the road" record, not so country as "I Walk the Line" and not as sappy as "Teenage Queen." It placed higher than ever on the pop charts, #11, and again was the #1 record on the country charts.

Events that took place soon afterwards made me wonder just what Johnny Cash expected of his record label. As we were celebrating the triumph of the new release, Sam heard a rumor that Cash had been approached by a major label. He asked Johnny if he was leaving Sun, and he denied it. Still, Sam believed his sources and was apprehensive that John would sign with Columbia when his Sun contract expired in August.

Johnny and his band went on the road immediately after Sam talked with him, and Sam sent Jud after him. I spoke with Jud the morning he arrived in North Dakota on John's coattails. I said, "What's it like in North Dakota?"

Jud replied, "This place is deserted. When you get out of the airplane you look around and say, 'Where's everybody?'" Then he told me of plans to locate John at the venue where he was playing and try to talk him into not leaving Sun. Jud had a very diplomatic, persuasive way about him, maybe partly due to his previous service as a chaplain in the Marine Corps. He could be a little smoother than Sam sometimes, and he was authorized to offer John a better royalty and more promotion support than he was already receiving. But it was too late. John admitted to Jud that, when he and Carl Perkins had gone to the West Coast the past November, Don Law had offered both of them Columbia contracts when their Sun obligations were over. Jud called both me and Sam to deliver the news.

For John, the attraction was not only a guaranteed $50,000 royalty the first year, but the chance to record the gospel album he had been itching to do. His royalty rate went from 3 to 5 percent of 90 percent of sales, and Columbia stressed they could give him greater possibilities for movies and TV. Word got around that he had a new manager, Stu Carnall, and perhaps this person had influenced John with dreams of bigger things to come. At one point, *Billboard* reported that he was having a screen test.

Jack Clement thought pride had something to do with Cash's leaving. Even though most of our artists were pals and supported each other in varying degrees, they were also competitive with each other. Jack Clement said John's feelings were ruffled because Sam had bought Carl Perkins a Cadillac for his million-seller, Sun's first, but not for him. John also believed Sam cared more for Jerry Lee Lewis and rock 'n' roll than John's country sound. Personal feelings could have influenced John, and Sam certainly took Cash's leaving personally. My feelings were ones of trepidation. I felt very bad for Sam personally and for the company. I also wondered if my future was in jeopardy. The record business and Sun at this moment didn't seem too stable.

Roy Orbison and Acuff-Rose

The Nashville music establishment had noticed with dismay and great resistance country's decline and the rise of rock 'n' roll. They had even just this spring formed a group called the Country Music Association to promote cohesion in the country field and to promote it more heavily. The RCA offices there had snapped up Elvis, and now Nashville was after another of our promising stars.

This time it was Roy Orbison. He had just returned from some dates on the road when next I saw him, and this time it was not just to hang around or practice, but to discuss an urgent matter with Sam. While he was touring, he had been on a bill in Indiana with the Everly Brothers. They had asked him if he had any songs to show them, and he obliged. Phil and Don especially liked and committed to record "Claudette," a song that Roy had written as a tribute to his wife.

A part of the deal was that the Everlys wanted him to go through Acuff-Rose publishing in Nashville, but he was under contract to Sun's publishing arm. They had just had a hit with "Bye Bye Love," and now they wanted "Claudette" for the B side of their new release, "All I Have to Do Is Dream." This development caused Roy to be more agitated than usual.

He came into my office exclaiming that he'd been trying to get in touch with Sam and Jud for about a week and they hadn't called him back. Through the Everly contact, he had met Wesley Rose of Acuff-Rose, and Rose asked him if he could break his songwriting contract with Sun and go with him. Roy was very insistent on speaking with someone who could make a decision about the matter.

When Jud called later that day, I told him Roy's complaint. Jud answered in an angry and sarcastic manner, "Tell him to can it or I'll come down there and knock that other eye cockeyed." I found Jud's response unhelpful and quite out of character.

Roy was still hanging around, so I told a little white lie and said Jud wasn't where I could reach him and that he should wait and talk to Sam. I wasn't in on the negotiations, but what it came down to in the end was that Roy bought out both his recording and songwriting contracts with Sun and went to Acuff-Rose, and that was the last we saw of Roy Orbison. The Acuff-Rose people got him a short-term recording contract with RCA Victor, but he didn't stay with them long, soon going to Monument and resuming his recording efforts.

A New Publication and a New Worry

My job at Sun had many facets, but my chief function was to be a salesperson. My task was to get our records noticed and played in as many ways as I could devise, using my telephone and typewriter. A new means of publicity was launched in May 1958 with the debut of *Sun-Liners*, a one-page monthly news sheet that contained information about our current releases. Sam as always had given me a free hand with content, saying I could include whatever I chose to feature, including mention of other labels' records. I laid out several boxes, with one devoted to a DJ spotlight, a couple mentioning new records (Cash and Lewis for the first issue), and a column of short news notes about our people, the industry at large, and whatever news I could find about DJs, stations, or others in our orbit. I even mentioned Roy Orbison's tune "Claudette" coming out on Cadence.

Tucked into the miscellaneous column was a note about Sam's appearance before a Senate committee looking into alleged abuses in TV and the recording industry. As it pertained to manufacturers, the issue was a practice known as *payola*, a term coined at the time to describe "pay for play," especially money paid to radio disk jockeys to play certain records.

Two senators, John McClelland and John Pastore, were prominent in the investigation, which was instigated in part by the music-licensing agency ASCAP, which alleged possible corruption and collusion between broadcasters and music publishers licensed through ASCAP's rival, BMI. ASCAP had long monopolized popular-music publishing, but with the growing importance of "fringe" music like hillbilly, blues, and especially rock 'n' roll, ASCAP was being left behind. Some in the organization were said to attribute the decline of their more traditional popular music to rock 'n' roll, which they saw as a fad that could be explained only by money, not popular acclaim.

Chairman Pastore accused several independent labels, including Aladdin, Chess, King, Modern, and Specialty, of engaging in payola. The hearings revealed that Syd Nathan of King Records and Lennie and Phil Chess of Chess Records entered their payoffs on their books and deducted them as business expenses. Most of the perks that the small DJs had enjoyed were modest—a bottle of whiskey here, fifty dollars there. The 1958 hearings centered on proposed legislation to outlaw payola, and they continued in 1959 with the involvement of another congressman, Oren Harris. Hearings were resurrected in 1960 after a notorious DJ convention in Miami.

The person who came off worst as a result of the hearings was Alan Freed. The Chess brothers had for a time kept him on their payroll as a "consultant," and Jerry Wexler of Atlantic had been delivering $500 a week to Freed at the Brill Building in New York in exchange for Freed's giving their records his "consideration." It was revealed that Bobby Darin had paid him $400 to be on a show Freed organized. The DJ-entrepreneur also was heavily into related ventures assuring him a cut of the profits of hit records. In 1958 twenty-four DJs were cited, and others were called to testify at various times. Strangely or not, none of those who made the news were ones I'd cultivated in my time at Sun.

Sam Phillips's 1958 testimony stressed that, even though Sun artists most often recorded BMI-licensed tunes, his radio station, WHER, played mostly ASCAP music. The only BMI company in which Sam's eleven corporations shared an interest was Jack Music, in which our songwriter and producer Jack Clement had a 25 percent interest.

Sam was very indignant about the whole issue and volunteered to appear so he could testify that Sun hadn't given payola and that the industry as a whole was clean. I didn't think Sam had been involved in payola, not only because of principle but because he wasn't inclined to give away money. Also, we had some great artists and hits, and the records from artists not so talented never made it to the charts. The issue of payola never once came up in my many, many phone calls with jocks and distributors.

Jud was very close to the Dick Clark organization, but I never heard of any allegations of collusion there. Dick Clark did divest some of his related companies as a result of the hearings, however. Jud had once told me he would occasionally peel off a hundred-dollar bill for a favorite DJ when they were out drinking. But, he said, "The jock would think 'Old Jud is drunk' and not consider the money a bribe." Some time later, we did issue a record that Alan Freed had a publishing interest in, but it bombed, so what did that prove? Actually, payola was not illegal when the hearings of 1958 and '59 took place, so it turned out that tax-evasion charges were the only serious legal ramifications of the hearings. The hearings had no effect on ASCAP or BMI, and the future would prove that rock 'n' roll was indeed not a fad but a trend.

Jerry Lee Alarms Great Britain

May 22, 1958, brought a momentous event that had enormous repercussions for Sam Phillips, Sun Records, and all of us who were in any way associated with the record company. The news that Jerry Lee Lewis had bigamously married his thirteen-year-old cousin, a story that had just broken in the British press, was the turning point that I believe eventually brought our little world of fun and music to a halt and scattered us to the four winds. The damage didn't appear irreparable at first, and things went on as usual for some time, but Sun never had a major star after this fiasco.

That morning, I got to work about 8:30 and immediately the phone rang, and it was Jud calling me from New York. He was already in the bar at the Manhattan Hotel, his home away from home. He said he had had a call late the night before from Helen Bolstad, a freelance popular-music writer, who got the news from London as soon as the Jerry Lee scandal broke. She came down to the hotel to find out the truth of the matter from Jud. She had often written about Sun artists, had been to Memphis visiting us, and we were supposedly friends all around.

Trying to avoid giving her the story she had come to ask about, Jud said with a rueful laugh, "I got poor old Helen drunk and then sent her back to her apartment in a taxi." The news was already breaking in the British tabloids, and it would soon be all over the U.S. media. Jud said reporters would quickly begin besieging us by phone for a statement. I was afraid they'd be bursting through the doors at any minute. Not knowing what to say and to avoid being trapped, I went home.

Even there, the phone rang almost immediately, but it was Sam. He said we needed to get together and write an open letter to the industry. We would buy space in *Billboard* and present Jerry in a better light. Sam explained more of what he had in mind, punctuating the reasonable content of his call with outbursts against "those hypocrites—those limeys" who had brought all this to pass.

Over the next week, we composed a contrite explanation and appeal for understanding, which ran June 9, but the few comments Jerry Lee had made before we got to him cancelled out any good will the ad might have engendered. In England, when asked about Myra Gale's age, he said, "She may be young, but she's a whole lot of woman." Just enough of an echo of "Whole Lot of Shakin'" to set off vivid images in the minds of some.

Jerry Lee told another reporter that he was in love with Myra and it was against his religious beliefs to have sex outside of marriage. Never mind that he had already had two wives, one of whom he married, with a metaphorical shotgun in his back, a little less than a month before his first divorce was final. Then he married Myra just before his second divorce came through. In the eyes of the law, he was a bigamist, an issue that eventually had Sam in the Memphis courts in Jerry Lee's behalf while Jerry was making his supposed-to-be-triumphal tour of England.

It wasn't just Myra's age that outraged the public, it was the incest angle. Myra's father, J. W. Brown, was not only Jerry's bass player, he was also a cousin. People felt that the "courtship" of the two young people could have hardly taken place without his complicity. Add to that the fact that, when Jerry Lee started living with J. W. and his wife, Lois, Jerry's second wife and their son were also there with him. Myra was the babysitter. If the press and general population needed greater confirmation of the decadence of rock 'n' roll, it needed look no further. Here was *Tobacco Road*, in living color, before the eyes of all to see.

Jerry Lee went on for the first three scheduled performances—he was contracted for thirty-seven nights—but was booed off the stage at each. So right away, Jerry and Myra winged it back to Memphis, where he was again met with an onslaught of press at the airport. He went into seclusion with the Browns.

Blame for the incident was rampant. Sam of course blamed the press. Jud blamed Jerry Lee and his manager, Oscar Davis. Oscar had elected to meet Jerry in London after a leisurely trip via luxury liner to London rather than flying with his charge. Jud had had misgivings about this potentially explosive situation since Jerry and Myra had walked blatantly through the lobby of the Manhattan Hotel some weeks earlier. "Even my kid Juddy could have done better in bringing a woman into a hotel than Jerry Lee Lewis," Jud raved. He had warned Jerry not to take Myra to England and thought Oscar should have prevented Myra from going and should have chaperoned Jerry Lee whenever he was in the public eye.

Since Jerry had secretly married Myra in a Mississippi ceremony (she said she was twenty) the previous December, he was convinced he was doing nothing wrong or even indiscreet in taking her to the New York hotel or even to England. He never seemed to acknowledge that there was anything weird about his marriage, and Myra herself stated later that she was more mature than her husband when they married. Besides, Jerry pointed out, she was really fourteen (lacking a couple of months), not thirteen, as the papers reported. He knew he was a celebrity, but he didn't know he could be brought down by public opinion.

In the meantime I was wondering what mixture of arrogance and ignorance caused Jerry Lee's downfall. Some of both, I decided, spawned by his upbringing in the poor and uneducated Lewis family in remote and impoverished Ferriday, Louisiana, the only world he really knew. He had no notion of what middle-class society considered proper, and even in Ferriday had not shown respect for convention or law, because aside from bigamy, he had committed other legal offenses in his youth. That was why his mother had sent him off to Bible college in Waxahachie,

Texas, but obviously the seminary and Jerry Lee's raucous piano playing couldn't get along. He was soon back in Ferriday, then on to Memphis, fame, and this debacle.

The Return of Jerry Lee

The entire population of the United States seemed to be outraged by the Jerry and Myra scandal, but some found the situation laughable. One of these was right there at Sun Records—Jack Clement. The weekend following all the hubbub, I went into the office to catch up on routine work I had neglected during the Jerry Lee crisis. Jack Clement was there with George Klein, one of Elvis's close friends and a frequent visitor at Sun. As he had so many times, Jack said, "Come here, B.B., I want you to listen to this."

I could hardly believe my ears. It was a tape with George Klein supposedly doing a remote broadcast from the Memphis airport, greeting Jerry Lee on his return from England. George would ask a question and Jerry's answer would be a phrase from one of his recordings. For example, to "How does it feel to be back in Memphis?" Jerry replied, "Feels good." When asked, "What did Queen Elizabeth say about your marriage?" the response was, "Great Balls of Fire!" Jack and Barbara Pittman had put together this piece of satire, which was clever but hardly an enhancement to the public perception of Jerry Lee's situation. Nevertheless, Sam chose to release it and it sold a few copies.

Jerry Lee's personal situation was far from humorous. He was banned on many stations and ignored by most. Dick Clark cancelled future bookings, and Jerry Lee's personal appearances became increasingly infrequent and very poorly paid. Elvis spoke out in his behalf when asked, but only Alan Freed, of all the visible media personalities, continued to play Jerry Lee and to offer a rationale of sort to Jerry's actions. He said people from the South were different, had their own peculiar views of marriage. In Jerry's case, it was definitely true.

MATCH BOX

YOUR TRUE LOVE

BLUE SUEDE SHOES

BOPPIN' THE BLUES

ALL MAMA'S CHILDREN

DANCE ALBUM OF ★ ★

CARL Perkins

Carl Perkins's debut Sun LP, *Dance Album of Carl Perkins*. His hit, "Blue Suede Shoes," deserved larger type on the cover. *Courtesy of Sun Entertainment Corporation.*

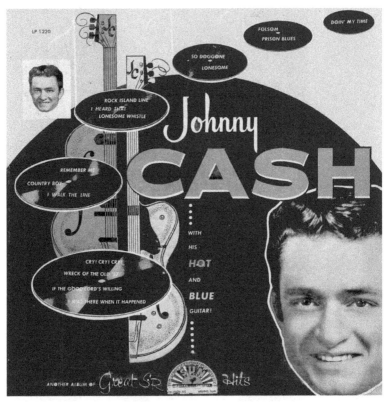

Johnny Cash's first album, *Johnny Cash with His Hot and Blue Guitar,* displayed his songwriting abilities. Backing by the Tennessee Two established the unmistakable Cash sound. *Courtesy of Sun Entertainment Corporation.*

SAM C. PHILLIPS

Sam Phillips, full of youthful confidence, left a radio career in Memphis for custom recording but found fame and wealth at his Sun Record Company, then branched out with Phillips International Corp. The new company's logo and a photo of Sam are included in an announcement brochure in the Sun exhibit at the Rock and Roll Hall of Fame. *Courtesy of Sun Entertainment Corporation.*

Colorful sales manager and Sam's brother, Jud Phillips. *Courtesy of Sun Entertainment Corporation.*

Bookkeeper and office manager Sally Wilbourn. *Courtesy of Sun Entertainment Corporation.*

Receptionist and office assistant Regina Reese. *Courtesy of Sun Entertainment Corporation.*

I took some Sun musicians to Webb Studio for their publicity photos, but in 1959 I had a sitting of my own. The times called for hat and gloves when a lady dressed up. *Author's collection.*

Music director and recording artist Bill Justis had the first hit on the Phillips International label, the trend-setting instrumental "Raunchy." *Courtesy of Sun Entertainment Corporation.*

Roy Orbison's pensive mood is apparent in this image, as well as in many of his songs. *Courtesy of the Roy Orbison Estate.*

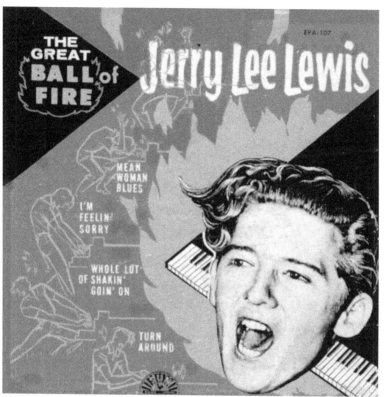

Jerry Lee Lewis's first EP referred to him as "The Great Ball of Fire." *Courtesy of Sun Entertainment Corporation.*

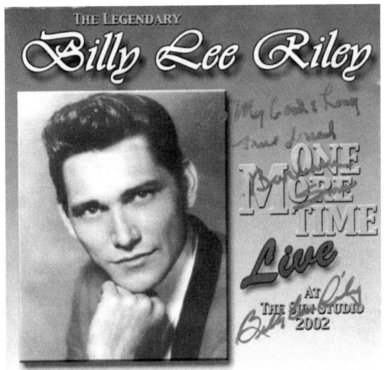

THE LEGENDARY
Billy Lee Riley

ONE MORE TIME
Live
AT THE SUN STUDIO 2002

Recorded Live At SUN STUDIOS, 706 Union, Memphis, TN

Billy Riley—singer, guitarist, bass man, and great showman—was omnipresent on Sun releases, as was his drummer, J. M. Van Eaton. *Courtesy of Sun Entertainment Corporation.*

Billy Riley's band, the Little Green Men. *Rear, left to right,* Jimmy Wilson, piano; Billy, guitar; J. M. Van Eaton, drums. *Front, left to right,* Pat O'Neil, bass, and Martin Willis, saxophone. *Courtesy of Sun Entertainment Corporation.*

Jerry Lee Lewis's "Breathless" was teamed with Beechnut Gum to sell more of both. The yellow Sun label is the most widely recognized label art in the world. The check mark was added to let DJs know this was the A-side. *The Sun Records logo is a registered trademark in the United States and elsewhere and is used by permission of Sun Entertainment Corporation.*

Jerry Lee with the stars of the MGM movie *High School Confidential*. The B side of the single was a good song, but the title was unfortunate in light of Jerry Lee's publicity debacle of 1958. *Courtesy of Sun Entertainment Corporation.*

jerry lee lewis 706 UNION AVENUE • MEMPHIS 3, TENNESSEE

Until his fan club got going, I answered Jerry Lee's fan mail on this stationery. *Courtesy of Sun Entertainment Corporation.*

SUN RECORD COMPANY
INCORPORATED

706 UNION   MEMPHIS, TENN.

SUN-LINERS

SUN STARTS SCANDAL SHEET

This is Vol. I, No. 1 of an official publication of Sun Record Company. We frankly admit being biased—since we expect to plug our new releases in said sheet. However, we're just as interested in featuring news about d. j.'s, distributors, other manufacturers, and persons otherwise connected with the recording industry. If you have an item—the editor, Barbara Barnes, would like to hear from you. Her address is 706 Union, Memphis—phone JAckson 7-7981.

Comment-able Items:

Congratulations to Roy Lamont of WRVA-TV, Richmond, who recently celebrated his second anniversary as m.c. of a very popular TV record hop. Roy tells us he's starting a new show—teaching dancing via TV . . . Also, congrats to KIOA on their first anniversary of broadcasting—they've achieved a lot in one short year . . . And best wishes to Ted Randle, KPIX-TV, in San Francisco, on his new dance party . . . At press time, Lew Chudd, Imperial president, was slated for a May 6 appearance before the committee considered the Smathers Bill. His position —that the public is not being maligned by a conspiracy among publishers, recording companies, and stations—is much the same as that taken by Sun president Sam Phillips, when he testified last month. The particular weight of Sam's testimony was this: his radio station, WHER in Memphis, was playing 79 per cent ASCAP music during their last audit in November 1956. And the policy hasn't changed . . . Memphis is one of the cities Jerry Shifrin visited during a recent sales tour for Roulette, in connection with his duties as national sales manager. We enjoyed having him in the city . . . Dick Biondi (WHOT, Youngstown) is one of the most enthusiastic supporters of a new Sun artist Edwin Bruce—and we love him! Ed's new release, (Sun 292) is SWEET WOMAN. We'd like to have your opinions on this one . . . Roy Orbison—who's under recording contract with Sun— is understandably elated over the success of his tune CLAUDETTE, recorded by the Everly Brothers on Cadence.

NEW SOUNDS

JACK CLEMENT makes his debut as a recording artist on Sun 291— TEN YEARS b/w YOUR LOVER BOY. A couple of weeks ago, we packaged up the records, sent them out, without saying too much about Jack —and much to our delight, TEN YEARS is getting a lot of reaction about the country, mostly in the medium-sized markets. It's hard to tell if Jack is a country artist who sounds sort of pop, or a pop artist who sounds sort of country. At any rate, we're counting on Jack to make it as an increasingly popular artist.

As a songwriter, Jack has already achieved a lot of prominence. He wrote both the tunes he recorded, and in addition has written a lot of Jerry Lee Lewis' material (including FOOLS LIKE ME—back side of HIGH SCHOOL CONFIDENTIAL, Sun 296). He also wrote Johnny Cash's biggest seller to date—BALLAD OF A TEEN-AGE QUEEN (Sun 283) and penned Johnny's latest release, GUESS THINGS HAPPEN THAT WAY (Sun 295). Imperial Records reports that Ricky Nelson is recording Jack's I'M FEELING SORRY.

So—the boy doesn't really HAVE to sing—he just likes to!

A word of special congratulations to

MILT GRANT

WTTG-TV personality, for his many successful activities in fields allied to the record industry. Particularly do we salute him for the work in combatting juvenile delinquency which won for Milt this month an award from the American Legion. A person such as Milt, who commands the attention and devotion of so many young people, is to be commended for channeling his efforts in such a constructive way.

For such a young man, Milt is a broadcasting veteran. He was in radio seven years before joining WTTG-TV in 1955. His Milt Grant TV record show was a pioneer show of its type and has copped a terrific rating. Milt's record hops have grown to gigantic proportions, covering Washington and surrounding area for a radius of 150 miles.

Jerry Lee Lewis
and
Johnny Cash Style

Latest release on the Sun label is Jerry Lee Lewis' rocking number HIGH SCHOOL CONFIDENTIAL (Boppin' at the High School Hop) (Sun 296). It gets its title from the MGM movie of the same name, in which Jerry appears in a featured role. None of us in Memphis have previewed the film—but Charles Felleman, who's coordinating promotion of the movie in New York—says Jerry plays his role to the hilt and comes through strong. To be world-premiered at Atlantic City, May 29.

Flip side is a sentimental ballad, FOOLS LIKE ME. This number is one of eight picked for Jerry's forthcoming LP. By the time you read this, the album should be on the market.

By the way, if you have any inquiries about the Jerry Lee Lewis National Fan Club, they should be addressed to Miss Regina Reese, 706 Union, Memphis.

Looks like Johnny Cash is in solid, judging from orders on his new ballad, GUESS THINGS HAPPEN THAT WAY. This number is genuine Cash material—simple, sort of philosophical, with a lonely quality.

The other side is COME IN, STRANGER. (Sun 295)

Our Sun newsletter told about our records, DJs, and other labels and artists. Here I mention that Ricky Nelson has recorded one of Jack Clement's tunes. *Courtesy of Sun Entertainment Corporation.*

THREE

---✦---

LATE 1958

Great Balls of Fire

JERRY LEE LEWIS (SUN 296)

Still stunned by Jerry Lee's flame-out, we soldiered on as the days length-ened into early summer 1958. The magnolias and crepe myrtles were beginning to bloom, and the many trees along the main streets and boulevards were in full leaf. It was warm, but the oppressive heat and humidity of July and August hadn't come yet.

Jerry Lee's "High School Confidential" was released as planned on June 2, to coincide with the appearance in movie houses of the film of the same name. We had a black-and-white sleeve to ship it in, showing a head shot of Jerry Lee with the stars of the movie in the background. The voluptuous Mamie Van Doren had the most eye-catching photo among the five cast members. In the movie, Jerry Lee, along with bass-ist J. W. Brown, his cousin and father-in-law, and drummer Russ Smith performed on the back of a truck, personifying the rock 'n' roll music that the teenyboppers loved and their parents hated. J.W. took the place of Roland Janes, who along with J. M. Van Eaton, had quit Jerry Lee's band at this time. However, in the movie, the music being heard was the original recording with Janes on guitar and Van Eaton on drums.

I was happily surprised that "High School Confidential" climbed to #21 on the charts. Its lyrics monotonously chanted, "Bopping at the high school hop" and was clearly a song "manufactured" for this movie.

I much preferred the country-sounding flip side, "Fools Like Me," which Jack Clement co-wrote.

Despite the ban that many radio and TV stations had imposed upon Jerry Lee, "High School Confidential" stayed on the *Billboard* Top 100 for eleven weeks. Some of Jerry's fans obviously loved him for his music and didn't think his personal life defined him. I kept thinking that, if the movie had featured a stronger song, Jerry Lee might have had a bona fide hit that would have put him back in the big arenas. As it was, just to keep him working, his manager had started booking small venues at a fraction of what he was making before he went to England.

Jud kept obsessing about ways to help Jerry make a comeback. He mentioned he'd like his writer friend, Helen Bolstad, or someone like her to do a fan-magazine piece with pictures of Myra and Jerry at home with their parents. "If they know more about him, show them cooking, playing with their dog, all that domestic stuff, they'll forget about the past. People do forget. We need to create a new impression of him."

He said he'd talked with Sam about some of his ideas, but Sam wasn't too interested. Even though he thought Jerry Lee had a chance to make it back in show business, Sam didn't have any ideas about how to help him. "Sam seems to have lost interest in the record business," Jud confided. "I'm about to lose my enthusiasm, too. Without that drive, you can't accomplish anything.

Newsletter Plugs

One encouraging sign, however, was that more and more mail began coming in as disk jockeys and some others on my mailing list began to respond to *Sun-Liners*, the golden one-sheet newsletter I had initiated in May to send to radio stations, trade papers, and our distributors. I had asked for news, and in response, I got letters from DJs in Minneapolis (Tom Lynn, WLOL), Seattle (Dave Neumann, KAYO), Youngstown (Dick Biondi, WHO), Cleveland (Bob Ancell and Phil McLean, WERE), Augusta, Georgia (Bob Ritter, WGUS), and many others, not all of whom I had space to recognize in the newsletter.

In July, we put out a similar newsletter for Phillips International, with the name *Scandal Sheet,* this one on white paper with blue type. Again, the jocks wrote in to report on how our releases were doing and to keep the industry abreast of what they were doing in their market or where they were moving, as DJs so often did. I noted in this issue that Bill Justis had "another entry in his catalog of nervous instrumentals." He called the tune "Cattywampus." Bill, in an ironic comment on trade-pub journalese, said I should say, "It's a new sound for Justis, featuring a soulful sax solo with a rock-solid beat." He played it on the ABC Saturday night Dick Clark show on July 26. The B side of "Cattywampus" featured a solo by Charlie Rich on celesta. The tinkly music of this small keyboard instrument was known to jazz fans, but was really a new sound for Sun.

Another Member of the Lewis Clan

When Sam told me we were getting ready to release a record by Jerry Lee's cousin, I thought, "Oh, my! What will this one look like?" I was pleasantly surprised when Carl McVoy appeared—personable, with nice manners, a cute face, and short curly hair.

I liked his voice, too. He sounded good, and different from Jerry Lee. I praised Carl in our release sheet for our distributors, urging them to stock the record. But I wasn't sure about the tunes, a country-rock number, "Tootsie," backed with the perennial Jimmie Davis tune, "You Are My Sunshine."

This was one of those rare times we released a record not cut in our studios. For $2,600, Sam had bought the master from Joe Cuoghi of Hi Records in Memphis, who had recorded it in Nashville with Chet Atkins. It had begun to sell regionally, and Sam liked it. I was thinking we'd have to sell many boxes of records to recover that up-front money plus sampling costs and the artist royalty of 3 percent. Possibly more for travel to promote it. It didn't look promising to me. We paid 14 cents to press a record, then sold it for 35 cents, so volume was the key.

Though he grew up in Arkansas, Carl was in part inspired to be a performer the same way Jerry Lee was, by watching the black entertainers who came to his uncle's nightclub in Ferriday, Louisiana. He was also related to Jerry's other cousins and musicians, the evangelist Jimmy Swaggart and Mickey Gilley, who sounded a lot like Jerry Lee in their singing and playing. Jerry Lee and Carl swapped visits in Arkansas and Louisiana as they were growing up.

About the same time Carl started coming in and cutting a few more tunes, Sam got a call from Audrey Williams asking if we had any good candidates to play her late husband, Hank Williams, in a proposed movie. He urged her to come to Memphis to look over Carl as a prospect. Never mind that he was a pianist, not a guitar picker.

Sam asked me to meet him at the Variety Club to help entertain Audrey. Carl told her about his experience with the Bill Black Combo and other work he'd done, and then he went to the piano to sing and play for her. He attempted a little patter between numbers, announcing he was going to do the honeymoon song, "It Don't Hurt Anymore." No yuks on that one. We drifted apart as the evening was ending, and the next day the word was out that Audrey had "auditioned" Carl privately at her hotel.

It was still early the next day when she came in and plopped herself down in my office. I just couldn't grasp that I was sitting three feet away from the woman who had inspired all those wonderful Hank Williams weepers. She wasn't old, in her mid-30s at the time, but her face showed many miles. Her heavy make-up and bleached hair cancelled out the positive appearance of her nice figure, and the girlish ruffles and flounces she was wearing were strangely incongruous with her jaded expression. Her conversation had a flat quality, as if she was there in body only.

After she went back to Nashville the next day, we never heard any more from her about the Hank Williams movie. Sam said in a sort of sheepish way that Audrey had indicated she wanted to "audition" him, too, but he wasn't willing to go that far to advance Carl's career. The tunes Jack had cut with Carl as a follow-up to "Tootsie" were never released, as the first record was a flop. But I remained a Carl McVoy fan, partly because in December, only he, among all our artists, thoughtfully sent me a Christmas card.

Elvis on Furlough

One day in early June something rather astonishing happened to me. I always imagined that if I ever met Elvis Presley, it would be at night, Elvis being the nocturnal creature of legend. As it was, I was heading through the studio to my little den, head down riffling through the day's mail, when I looked up and saw that I was within a foot of the back of a man in uniform. Sam, facing me, was deep in conversation with this figure.

Sam stopped me and said, "Barbara, I would like you to meet Elvis Presley."

Elvis stuck out his hand and said, "Glad to meet you, ma'am."

I managed to contain my surprise and asked Elvis if he were enjoying his visit home from Fort Hood, and he said he was. We exchanged a couple of other pleasantries and I excused myself. I would have liked to talk with him some more, but the other part of my brain said it wasn't polite to intrude, especially with someone as constant prey as Elvis.

Still, I fully took in what a beautiful sight to behold the real Elvis Presley was that day. He no longer fit the stereotype that had been attributed to him—a sneering hillbilly cat with a pompadour, purple jacket, and teenager skin. Instead, I saw a fit and glowing specimen of manhood with a neat haircut and custom-tailored uniform that showed off his perfect physique. He looked me squarely in the face in a sincere manner as he said he enjoyed meeting me, and I thought he had a lovely smile, with some warmth and humility shining through. What a dish!

The papers were full of news about his leave, his skating parties, his gang of friends who went everywhere with him, his girlfriend Anita Wood. He was of endless interest to everyone in Memphis and, judging from magazine covers I saw on newsstands, everywhere else, too.

Getting Some Wheels

I was still longing to buy my first car. My bank account was slowly growing, and I asked Jud for advice about buying a used car. A couple of weeks later, he brought a big green Buick from Florence, Alabama, that he said a dealer friend of his wanted to sell. It was too much car and it cost too much, but I did want to take it to Motor Vehicles and get a Tennessee driver's license.

I had been driving since I was sixteen, so passing the written test was a breeze, but when it was time for the test drive, the examiner refused to let me drive. He stated that, since the car wasn't registered in my name, it might be stolen. Me, a car thief? Wow! I had taken driving tests in cars belonging to other people when I got licenses in Mississippi and Louisiana, so I couldn't understand this pipsqueak's refusal to let me take the driving test. It was a big deal getting there for the test—taking time off work, borrowing a car, and driving clear across Memphis.

I didn't buy the car and I didn't get the license, but later I told my landlady about my situation, and she had a friend who was planning to sell her car. I took it for a test drive to the Sun studios, where I asked Sam to drive it and check it out for me. He said it seemed to be fine and that the $400 the owner was asking was fair. Soon I was the proud owner of a black 1949 Chevrolet sedan. Having wheels and a little more in my bank account now, I was also able to move into an apartment and found a congenial roommate in Sandra Pirtle, who was also a University of Alabama alum and who worked in public relations for the National Cotton Council.

Now my thoughts were turning to graduate school. Before I went to work with Sun, I had investigated returning to the University of Alabama for an advanced degree in radio-TV, but I couldn't swing it financially. So I had decided to study English part-time at Memphis State, which had a campus about ten miles from downtown. I enrolled for the summer semester in a course on Chaucer and one on southern literature. One was offered at 7:30 a.m., and the other at 7 p.m., Tuesday and Thursday. I thought I could manage that.

My Chaucer teacher was wonderful, but the southern lit class was taught by a prig. Early in the semester when we were discussing the ballad tradition, I brought him a copy of Jack Clement's single, "Ten Years," which we had issued in April. I was excited to tell him that right here in Memphis a singer and guitar player was carrying on that strain of English music. He took the disk rather gingerly and never again mentioned it or spoke to me personally, so it seemed I had committed a grave faux pas. I gathered it had to do with "high culture" and "low culture," and current recordings were a bit vulgar or embarrassing to highly educated people like this fellow. His condescending attitude was pretty widespread in Memphis.

For the next two years, at night and on Saturday mornings, I took courses in English, with several in European history for my minor. I liked the rest of my teachers OK except the American lit teacher who consistently ignored the women in the class. On one or another occasion, he would address a remark to, "You bright young men who are going to be the professors of tomorrow." And of course there were no women professors among my teachers the entire time.

The Stars of Country Music

Despite Sun's reputation as a rock 'n' roll label, we featured country songs on the back of our major rock releases, and some of our artists like Johnny Cash and Warren Smith were clearly country singers. Jerry Lee, whose recent calamitous decline would ultimately lead to a new identity with country music, had recorded some great country sides, like "You Win Again" and "Crazy Arms." I had contacts with many country stations and DJs. When a buzz started up about a country DJ convention in Nashville that summer, I naturally assumed that I would be going.

As the time grew closer, however, Sam didn't say anything about my going. I heard through Sally that Sam intended to go alone. That surprised me, because Sam didn't like attending public gatherings. In this case, though, he could drive to Nashville, not have to fly, and he knew his way around, having worked there. But I was disappointed to be left behind.

The day of the convention rolled around and sure enough, Sally, Regina, and I were alone in the office. Bill and Jack had apparently taken off to Nashville on their own. We "girls" were taking a day off, too, gossiping, and I was filing my nails when the phone rang on the Phillips International line where I received and made most of my calls. Amidst a roar of conversation in the background, I heard, "Barbara, this is Sam Phillips. I'm here at the Andrew Jackson hotel with Ren Grevatt from *Billboard* magazine. He wants to meet you."

Of course I knew the name because I had been talking with Ren every week since January. One of my jobs was to cultivate the trade-journal personnel who were responsible for reviewing records, and Ren was on the R&B desk. When I was in New York with Jud earlier that year, we had missed Ren when we dropped in at the *Billboard* offices. Sam continued in his formal radio-announcer voice, "How soon do you think you can get over here?"

I answered, "I can leave right away, so I should be able to get there in early afternoon." It was a two-hundred-mile drive, and the new interstate highway system hadn't come to Tennessee yet. With all the small-town red lights, weaving my way through Nashville, parking, and everything else, I figured it would take about four hours. I left almost immediately, and before too long I was in the cool hotel lobby of the Andrew Jackson Hotel with Sam and Ren, whom I found to be personable and attractive.

We discussed how he conducted the weekly meetings with *Billboard* to select its "picks" from among the releases they had just received from the manufacturers like us or the New York distributors. According to Ren, several staff members would listen to the recordings and then discuss what they liked or didn't like about them. I was envious of Atlantic's Ahmet Ertugan and Jerry Wexler, who Ren said would often attend these sessions. I am sure they picked up some good ideas about the market that way, as well as hearing artists they might want to pluck up for their label.

On the convention floor there seemed to be a congregation of rare birds in their courting plumage. Quite a few of the country DJs and musicians had come out in their green, pink, and powder-blue fitted suits spangled with rhinestones. Even those in conventional suits or sport coats had boots—pointed toes, high heels, with all types of skins including alligator and ostrich. It was close to breathtaking!

I enjoyed meeting another trade-journal bigwig, Charlie Lamb of the Nashville-based *Music Reporter*. I depended on Charlie hugely to get the word out about our country sides, as those records tended to take a back seat to our rock 'n' roll releases. Charlie Lamb had founded this magazine in 1956. He was well named, lovable as a lamb, speaking in a soft Knoxville-inflected accent that belied the colorful and high-powered role he played in country music. Over the phone he sounded like a small man, and indeed he was hardly more than my five-foot-five-inch height. But I had heard that he had a huge imagination and drive and was a powerful figure in the development of the Nashville music industry. He, like Col. Tom Parker, had earlier been a part of the circus world: Charlie's mother was an aerialist, his father an animal trainer. Charlie was at one time a barker, or "talker" as they would say in that world.

In Nashville he wore or had worn many hats: sales rep for *Billboard* and *Cashbox,* Mercury record-label promotion man, booking agent for live shows, talent manager, you name it. He brought innovative ideas to the *Music Reporter.* It was the first trade paper to use the bullet feature, indicating that a record showed strong signs of rapidly climbing high in the charts. He also initiated the Top 100 list, which was copied by the other trade magazines. When I asked him about himself, I didn't expect to learn so much, but it was all interesting. I invited him to visit us in Memphis, and later he did.

I only stayed the day and headed back to Memphis that night. The drive seemed much longer and lonelier in the dark, but it gave me time to marvel about the great diversity of the business as it had been shown to me in this convention, just as it had in my trips to Chicago and New York.

Johnny Cash Farewell Sessions

As soon as Cash confirmed that he had signed with Columbia and was moving to the West Coast in August, Sam determined to get the most he could from the remainder of his contract. A marathon session in May and one in July were booked, but with a lack of enthusiasm on the part of Johnny Cash. He continued to be friendly with Jack Clement, but when he strode through the office, Cash did so with a very aloof bearing and a grim countenance. Regina termed his erect carriage and blue-black hair "dramatic," but besides that quality, I saw stiff-necked Anglo-Saxon pride.

He had what appeared to be a scar on his left check, which made him look a little dangerous and mysterious.

Jack Clement could be counted on to write some original material for the sessions, and a new songwriter that Bill Justis was working with, Charlie Rich, was also recruited for this effort. Charlie had studied music at the University of Arkansas and was well qualified to prepare lead sheets to go with some of our releases, as well as playing piano on sessions. He even played piano on some of Jerry Lee's records when the chord patterns were too complex for the Killer.

We were getting used to seeing Charlie quietly noodling at the piano, and he was ready with some Cash material. Johnny was reluctant to record his own new songs, intending them to launch his Columbia career. We didn't doubt that Johnny would perform well, because he didn't want any bad records out there any more than we did.

Sam was not only determined to call Cash in for the number of sessions specified in his contract, but also to capitalize on single sales before Columbia could get any product on the market. While "Guess Things Happen that Way" was still selling, we put out one Charlie Rich had written for him, "The Ways of a Woman in Love," in late May. Sun continued to issue Cash singles through the remainder of 1958 into 1960. Some, if not most, were only moderately memorable, but when both Sun and Columbia had entries on the charts, we sometimes were ahead.

Early in the summer, we also put out the first of several extended-play albums on John, and I thought it was quite a good one—*Johnny Cash Sings Hank Williams* (EPA 111). The content consisted of four numbers, and the disk looked just like a 45, but it had more grooves. We used a hard cover with Johnny in concert on the front, and it looked nice. The initial orders were for 17,500 albums, impressive enough to warrant a notice in the trade papers.

I could see phenomenal growth in Johnny Cash as an artist in the year that I had observed him and listened to his music. For one thing, he was learning how to relate to an audience. When Jud accompanied him to New York for the Dick Clark show in July, I wasn't worried about how he would handle being on camera. For earlier shows, I had suggested to Jud that he try to get the producers to have him shown with waist or face shots, because he was so rigid. Whether it was stage fright, inexperience, or an intrinsic inhibited nature, in those days he seemed to move only his mouth and his fingers on the guitar strings when he performed. Being so tall, he almost looked like a statue, and a rather grim one at that.

His problem had been the opposite of Elvis's. The reason Ed Sullivan wanted that dynamo photographed from the waist up was because of his gyrations. Cash was getting more animated now, so full-body shots could be effective. He was smiling more, kicking up his heels a bit. He would never be a particularly graceful man, I thought, but he was loosening up so that he could enjoy audiences and they could enjoy him.

Back in my little office, I had grown accustomed to the sounds of Johnny Cash and his sessions. Marshall Grant's bass came through the walls in its steady beat even when that's all that I could hear. Cash's recording dates during his last months with Sun had yielded ample material for release, and Sam notified the market of this fast. We were certainly going to miss Johnny Cash because we all thought he was a great talent. Sam said he had more depth than most of the other artists he had worked with and great potential personally and professionally.

Boys Will Be Boys

Hayden Thompson was one of the artists released on the initial pressings of Phillips International Records but who, unfortunately, never became a household word. I interviewed him for the pamphlet I wrote for the label's debut and learned he was from Booneville, Mississippi, just down the road apiece from my home in Corinth. He said that he, like Jerry Lee, had sold eggs his mother accumulated from raising chickens in order to finance his first trip to Memphis. He found studio sideman work at Sun through playing the clubs with Billy Riley's band. He had high hopes for his first record, but it fizzled. The second time I recall encountering Hayden concerned a moment when he and Jack Clement came close to blows.

The band wasn't there—it was just Hayden alone at the microphone going through some tunes, trying with Jack Clement to work up something for his next session. The guys said that Jack sometimes liked to goad musicians to make them do their best, and I don't know if that was his strategy that day or what. Anyhow, he must have said something Hayden took exception to, because what I heard coming out of the mike was Hayden shouting, "Ain't no son of a bitch in short pants gonna talk to me that way."

Hayden was referring to Jack's Bermuda shorts, a rare costume for men in the mid-South in those days, and certainly not one you'd see in a place of business. Jack was in what we called his "Dr. Livingston" period, with a safari helmet to match the pants. I rushed out of my office and through the studio partly out of curiosity and partly in hopes my sudden appearance would forestall physical blows. Hayden quieted down, and soon they were working on songs again.

The only other time I heard of Jack's almost getting into an altercation with a musician concerned Billy Riley. It had to do with one of Jack's efforts to attract the opposite sex. Jack had been married and divorced (a pretty lady named Doris was his ex) by the time I arrived at Sun, and he was thinking a lot about girls. Sam had driven up one day with a head of wavy bright blond hair, a striking change from his normal brown color. So Jack decided to go blond, too. His transformation was actually more effective, as the bleach job was more subtle. He was also considering growing his hair long. "Chicks dig long moss," he told us, though, as time went on, he didn't let his hair grow nearly as long as Sam did his.

On the other hand, when he decided his nose wasn't his most attractive feature, he did something about it. Elvis had had a nose job and had paid for his friend, the sleek and voluble George Klein, to have an elegant new nose, too. I thought Jack's nose was fine, a good Gallic nose as befit his ancestry. But he went in for plastic surgery, and when Regina and I visited him in the hospital, we found him swathed in bandages over much of his face. When they came off, he looked fine, but I couldn't tell much difference.

It was the nose job that was the focus of the narrowly averted fight with Billy Riley. The pugnacious Riley took offense at something Jack said during a session and charged into the control room for a fight. Jack backed off, "No, man. My nose, watch my nose." It had barely had time to heal, and Jack was terrified that the surgical efforts would be destroyed. I wasn't there when this event happened, but Billy loved to tell that story ever after.

Besides being the day-to-day musical contact that our musicians looked to, some of them depended on Jack for their nighttime entertainment. Jack had an apartment not far from the studios where he welcomed the musicians to "orgies," which when I heard them described (I was never invited to one) seemed to be more like frat parties. We girls weren't privy to many details, but the events seemed to involve some drinking and adolescent pranks, such as jumping into the pool from the roof.

Jack and various others in the Sun crowd had motorcycles, and I have heard that the guys—even Elvis in times past—sometimes went for nude bike rides. Nudity seemed to be a big thing. Roy Scott, dignified lawyer though he was, attended one of the parties and reported seeing Jerry Lee Lewis sitting atop a refrigerator in the altogether.

An accumulation of annoyances and complaints from other tenants moved the landlord to decide he no longer required Jack as a tenant. Far from being nonplussed, Jack considered being evicted some kind of accomplishment and proudly showed me a copy of his eviction letter. Then he got a house far from Union Avenue and asked me to help him shop for furniture, which I enjoyed doing. At that point, Jack's role as party host toned down considerably.

On many Sunday nights, he still joined up with George Klein and other friends but to go to East Trigg Baptist Church, which reserved an area in the back of the church for young whites who came regularly to drink in the sounds of the church's spirited gospel singers and musicians. The Reverend Herbert Brewster, who sang, wrote songs that had been million-sellers, and preached the gospel, presided over a black congregation that indeed could make a joyful noise.

Plans for a New Studio

Summer also brought a major development to Sun Record Company. At opening time one Monday morning (this was the day he usually got there early), Sam arrived in a buoyant mood, eager to convey the good news that he'd bought property at 639 Madison for a new studio. He exclaimed that we would have ample space for staff offices, as well as great new equipment and two studios for greater technical flexibility in recording. We were going to be an even greater record company and now, custom recording studio! He had hired a renovations manager and decorator, and work would begin soon on the remodeling of the building he had bought.

At noon, some of us traveled the short distance over to Madison to take a look, and we could see it was a great location, but the building needed a lot of work outside. Naturally, the inside would have to be entirely redone, because it was a former wholesale bakery. There would be room for parking, which was a great improvement.

The leased 706 location had certainly served well as a place to generate hits, and we managed to conduct our business there, but the idea of greater comfort and a place to park was really welcome. Despite his other business interests, Sam intended to keep making records, though he had doubts that rock 'n' roll would always be so popular, and now he could afford better quarters. One day some months past, Sally had looked up from her bookkeeping and announced, "Sam has a million dollars in his bank account." I wasn't surprised, because the figure three million had been floated as an estimate of our annual gross. I didn't know much about the money flow, but I was up to date on sales, which had been great since before I arrived. I also knew that expenses had to be low, with our staff so small and no one making a high salary.

Sam's greatest expectation for the new facility lay in custom recording and mastering. Ever on the lookout for a good investment (he hadn't done badly sinking some cash in Holiday Inns), he felt Memphis was a magnet for the abundant indigenous talent, and that there was no real competition in recording. One studio, the Pepper facility, was making commercials, but that market had room for competition, and only a few obscure studios were putting out records. But Sam envisioned the Sam C. Phillips Recording Studios as something comparable to the Nashville facilities where almost all of America's country music was produced.

Sam could even compete with them, as the Sun label had always had a country catalog.

A Wink and a Smile

By July, even though I had been associated with Sun only a year, I felt as if those of us who worked together had established real bonds. I looked forward to seeing everyone each day because the people were all my friends and the mix was entertaining. Among the many who drifted in, there were those whose presence was consistent. I could always count on Regina for companionship and gossip at lunch. Jack Clement was a continual source of entertainment and fun. Bill Justis's wry commentary on current happenings was amusing. And we tried to help each other in small ways, as Bill Justis did once when I commented that I couldn't get through to our local TV host, Wink Martindale.

Wink's show, the "Top Ten Dance Party," aired on WHBQ-TV. His looks fit the Dick Clark stereotype perfectly—earnest wide-set eyes, perfect teeth, and a voice that oozed confidence and warmth. Wink also had wavy hair with a bit of a receding hairline, leaving a nice widow's peak. He had come up through radio, starting in his hometown of Jackson, Tennessee. Like Carl Perkins and me, he had worked for Aaron Robinson's Dixie network station, in their case WDXI in Jackson. Wink, short for Winston, hooked up in Memphis with promoter and former Elvis manager Bob Neal, and sometimes was the emcee for his Stars Inc. live shows that often featured our artists.

I couldn't understand why I could get through to similar dance-show hosts coast to coast but couldn't get Wink on the phone to ask him to play our records. When I mentioned this to Bill, he said, "Oh, you want to talk to Mr. Ho-Hum? We could take Winkie out to lunch—I'll ask him." Bill's name was known to Wink, so he took the call and accepted Bill's invitation. He even offered to pick us up at the studio.

I dressed up for the occasion, even donning what I thought was a smart white feathered hat. Bill as usual had something ironic to say. "B.B., what have you got on your head? It looks like a frustrated chicken."

But these little jibes were endearing, no malice there, just letting me know he noticed.

Things got off to a good start with my admiring Wink's shiny Thunderbird and congratulating him on his high ratings in the market. But I put my foot in my mouth by saying that, after all my attempts to reach him, it was good to meet him. I didn't say it sarcastically, but he immediately clouded with anger. He demanded, "Is that what you tell Sam Phillips?" Apparently, Sam's opinion was significant to him. Bill Justis leapt in with a witticism that smoothed the situation. But I never felt comfortable approaching Wink after that, and soon he left Memphis for Los Angeles and bigger things at KJH. I did give him a couple of plugs in future newsletters, once noting that his record, "Deck of Cards," had made it to #7 on the *Billboard* charts.

Jack Clement Takes the Mike

In a late-1958 issue of the Phillips International *Scandal Sheet,* I spotlighted an exciting single, "Tom Dooley," that Capitol had issued by the Kingston Trio. The Bay Area group sang an updated version of an old North Carolina ballad, recorded with an energetic guitar and banjo backing. It eventually made it to #1 on the *Billboard* charts.

The success of "Tom Dooley" encouraged me to think that Jack Clement might have a chance with the emerging folk-music audience that I had read was forming in New York's Greenwich Village and a few other scattered locations. In April, Jack had recorded "Ten Years," which had a ballad feeling, and in November he had traveled to RCA's Nashville studios to get the sound he wanted on his second release, "The Black Haired Man." He produced both records, but while in Nashville he renewed acquaintance with Chet Atkins, the celebrated finger-picking guitar pioneer and "Nashville Sound" producer, who incidentally felt him out about working for him at RCA.

"Ten Years" didn't catch on, but we hoped the next release would do better. For "The Black Haired Man," I prepared a special flyer intended to depict both the collegiate and country-folk sides of Jack. Bill and Joy

Webb, a husband-and-wife team we patronized when we needed nice pictures made, photographed him sitting beside a large rustic-looking fireplace that conveniently happened to be in the apartment Sandra Pirtle and I were renting at that time. He was wearing an L. L. Bean–looking plaid shirt and khakis. We had gone to Julius Lewis to get the shirt, and I suggested the button-down collar, hoping that this would look both a little preppy and a little country with the plaid. He got a nice haircut that showed off his wavy hair, but I had neglected to mention shoes, and I thought the effect was marred a little by the sandals he showed up in. The photos turned out to be just right for the outside of the flyer, which bore the legend, "Inside Lies the Story of the Black-Haired Man," with "Sun 311" in the corner. We got nice reviews in the trades and a great feature article in the Memphis paper.

I bore down so hard on our distributors to buy the record that Willie Roessner, the promo man for our Kansas City distributor, asked me if Jack were my boyfriend. Some of the pop stations put it on their lists, as did several country stations, but the record just didn't take off. As with Bill Justis and his releases, Jack couldn't leave his day-to-day job in the studio to go on the road for the exposure. Whether this promotion would have helped, I can't say, but as it was, the record was a big disappointment.

It was ironic that Jack had written hits for Cash and Lewis and other songs for Roy Orbison and others, but he couldn't find many listeners for his own work. But he had so many irons in the fire I wasn't worried that his records didn't become hits.

Death of Gladys Presley

August brought sad news to those of the Sun family who had been a part of the launch of Elvis Presley as the hottest young entertainer in America. Elvis Presley's mother, Gladys, died on August 14, bringing the young star a loss that haunted him during his own short life. Gladys was only forty-six when she died, but she had been in poor health for a long time.

Elvis was in Memphis on emergency leave from Fort Hood when she passed away, but had gone home from the hospital to Graceland for a short rest. From the time he received the call about his mother's death, Elvis was beside himself with grief. This news was brought to us by some buddies who had been with him at Graceland. Far from respecting the family in their time of mourning, throngs gathered at Graceland, Memphis Funeral Home, and Forest Hill Cemetery for a glimpse of Elvis and the events surrounding the funeral and burial.

At home, Elvis found little consolation in the presence of the friends who gathered there. Sally reported that Elvis's dad, Vernon, had asked Sam to come and talk to Elvis. When it came time for the body to be moved from Graceland for the funeral service, Elvis was so bereaved that he refused to let the funeral home take Gladys's casket. He had been sitting beside it in a state of near-paralysis for two days, utterly desolate.

Sam's early experience in Alabama working in a funeral home had prepared him for situations like this one. Elvis trusted him, and Sam could be very persuasive. According to Sally, Sam talked with Elvis several hours and finally convinced him to go to bed and rest and to allow the body to be removed the next morning so that services could be held as scheduled.

During the funeral and burial service, he struggled to accept that the great love of his life was gone. At the interment, Cliff Gleaves told us later, Elvis became very emotional when her casket was lowered into the ground. He was near collapse, and they believed he would never be the same again because his mother's demise seemed more than he could bear.

Considering Charlie Rich and Losing a Sales Manager

Jud was in town, though I didn't know if he had come in for Mrs. Presley's funeral or just to take a break from traveling, and when he came into the office, it was a chance for me to find out what the plans were for a new artist I was particularly taken with.

"Charlie Rich has been coming in a lot, writing for Cash. But I've heard him sing, and he sounds good to me. If we got a strong record and you gave him a big push, I bet he could make it," I said. I didn't add that I was getting very worried about Cash, Lewis, and Orbison being either gone or commercial poison. How long could the back catalog keep us afloat?

Jud said, "Sam doesn't want that. He doesn't want to promote him as an artist. Charlie is a good songwriter and Sam wants him to concentrate on that."

"Well, I can't see that he has to do just one or the other," I objected. This sounded like Roy Orbison all over again, I thought in disgust.

"I'm not too sold on him, either," Jud said. "I don't like his looks." True, Charlie didn't look like a teen idol exactly, rather brawny instead with a streak of white running through his hair. To me, this was sort of romantic.

Unfortunately, Jud wasn't going to be around to see if Charlie Rich could make it as an artist, because he and Sam had a disagreement that led to his departure from Sun Records. Sam didn't say anything about it to me, but Jud later told me that he had asked Sam for the financial settlement they had agreed upon when he went on the road, and Sam refused to pay him what Jud felt was due. "Sam said I'd already spent my part," Jud avowed.

Cookie and the Cupcakes

Even though he was no longer an employee, Jud was not gone from the scene. He made a personal management deal with Jerry Lee and continued to book and promote him. He also had lingering hopes of remaining attached to Sun through some artists he wanted to get recorded. One afternoon I walked in on a conversation in which he was pitching some of them to Sam. None of the names meant anything to me as he reeled them off, but for every one that he proposed, Sam would shake his head. The one Jud was hyping the most had a whimsical name, Cookie and the Cupcakes.

Jud was saying that they were an R&B, or what I later heard called swamp-pop, group from Lake Charles, Louisiana, and that they'd had good radio play and sales in the area around the Louisiana and Texas border. Jud thought that with the right recording and promotion, they could generate national sales and compete with East Coast doo-wop groups.

Jud had been booking them as an opening act for Jerry Lee's shows, and they could grab a crowd, he said. He continued, stressing that they had a good beat for dancing and were a well-behaved group. "You won't have any trouble with these guys, they're professionals," he said.

Sam again shook his head to signify a categorical "no."

"So you don't want—" and then repeated the names of all the acts he was pushing, concluding with "and you don't want Cookie and the Cupcakes." Jud stated this ironically, with a look of disdain on his face to convey how pigheaded and wrong his brother could be.

Jud and Sam were a great team, each without peer in his specialty in selling records. But their relationship was always at the point of eruption. I thought perhaps there was a strong element of sibling rivalry in their relationship. In fact, once Jud told me he wasn't the favored son—Sam was. At the same time, I recognized an unbreakable bond of blood and love, as well as respect for the talents of the other.

I really hated to see Jud go, both for me, because I liked working with him, and for the company. What would we do without him? At one time Jud had suggested to Sam that he put me on the road, but Sam didn't go for the idea at the time, and neither did I. I definitely couldn't assume his role, and there was no one else on the horizon. The promotion I did in the office was important, but it was Jud who dealt with the big entertainment figures and who knew the business.

Not too long after this conversation, a 45 record showed up in the office with a blue label bearing the name JUDD. I had heard rumors Jud was starting his own label, and here was the proof—"Mathilda," by Cookie and the Cupcakes. It had a beat for dancing and wailing lines that were easy to sing along with. It made it to #47 on the *Billboard* charts, and Jud booked them on American Bandstand and on an Alan Freed tour. They continued to open for Jerry Lee, and put out a follow-up to "Mathilda," but they never did make it big.

Merry Christmas, Baby

December rolled around, the Salvation Army bell ringers took their places at store entrances, the decorated lamp posts glittered in the early dusk, and it began to get really cold. Regina answered the phone, "Merry Christmas, Sun Records."

The grouchy postman brought us cards and gifts from among our many contacts. My favorite by far was from George Struth, production coordinator of Quality Recording Limited, the company that represented our lines in Canada. The box arrived with a card on yellow paper with red printing that said, "Enclosed with our best wishes is one lambskin rug. Trust you will send appropriate photograph of rug, person and fireplace. Merry Christmas. Personal Regards, G." I was some years past the time of having my baby picture in the nude on a woolly rug, but I did find the gift a cozy spot in front of the fireplace in the apartment my roommate Sandra and I shared.

Sandra and I decorated a tall Christmas tree in our apartment, inspired by songs pealing from the record shops along Main Street and the elaborate decorations in the windows of Goldsmith's and other downtown department stores. But at 706 Union, we had a little bobble in efforts to have a proper celebration.

Regina and I asked Sally for money to buy a Christmas tree, but she reported that Sam refused our request, saying we could use the tree from last year that was in the storage room. Digging among the boxes of returns, we retrieved it. The tree had been fresh once, but now it was truly disgusting—brown with needles falling off. But Sam said to use it, so we did. It was about two feet tall, just the size for a table we brought to the front office. For decorations, we used whatever was at hand. Jack and some of the musicians helped Regina and me hang on paper clips, old pink memos, cigarette butts, a broken 45, and any other trash we could find. For the tip-top instead of a star we placed an empty beer can.

The next morning Sally reported that Sam was very disgusted and angry, demanding in profane language that we get rid of that sick Christmas tree immediately. He wasn't Scrooge entirely, though, because the day before Christmas he came in laden with gifts for everyone, including a nice blue wake-up-to-music portable radio for me.

FOUR

✦

1959

Guess Things Happen That Way

JOHNNY CASH (SUN 295)

The first Monday in 1959 marked my first anniversary as a full-time Sun employee, and I was happy there despite the reversals Sun had endured in 1958. I really enjoyed the work, and I liked being among creative and endlessly amusing people. I sometimes thought that musicians were just big children and Sun Record Company was their playpen. Sam possessed generosity of spirit, giving us a lot of freedom to do our jobs and appreciation of our efforts. But I dreaded going to work on that Monday, because it was so cold. The temperature had dropped to 9 degrees in the early morning hours, and it took a long time for my trusty '49 Chevy to warm up for my commute.

I knew my feet would stay cold all day, even in my bobby socks and loafers. Sam had made a remark about them on another cold day, saying, "I never saw a woman your age wear bobby socks." He added he liked baby-doll pumps on women, but he didn't say my loafers were forbidden, so I kept wearing them, with my socks, because the floors at the studio were so very cold. In fact, the whole building was flimsy and drafty, and there was no way to heat it sufficiently when temperatures got below freezing. I had a space heater in my office that Jack Clement would sometimes back up to in an attempt to thaw out from the cold in the control room.

That Monday, January 5, also happened to be Sam's birthday, and as had become our custom during the year I had been aboard, this event called for a little office party. There had to be a cake, of course, and a small gift for which we took up a collection. I suggested sparkling burgundy, and that seemed pleasing to everyone. Sally doled out funds for the refreshments from petty cash, and we took turns collecting the money and shopping for a suitable card and gift.

I was usually the one who went downtown to get the cake from a bakery near the Peabody Hotel. On this occasion, I searched in vain for a parking space, so I stopped my car in front of the bakery door and hailed a black man who was passing by and who looked friendly enough. I asked him if he would mind going in to get the cake for me. He looked slightly puzzled but said OK, so I gave him the six dollars and waited for him to return. I waited and waited, waited some more, and finally it dawned on me that he wasn't coming back. Darn!

I didn't have enough money to get the cake myself, so I went back and asked Sally for more petty cash. She gave me a skeptical look but did give me more money. When she told Sam, he said, "That sounds just like Barbara." But he was more amused than annoyed, and by five o'clock we had everything set for a nice little time together. It was Sam's thirty-sixth birthday. Everyone else in the company was younger than Sam. Bill was in his thirties, and the rest of us were in our twenties. Birthdays were still events we looked forward to.

Charlie Rich Makes His Own Recordings

Charlie Rich had been coming in for a while playing on sessions, writing songs, and working with Bill Justis with the goal of becoming a recording artist himself instead of always being in the supporting role. In fact, he had had a release the previous summer, though Sam wasn't all out for the idea. It was one of those songs I called "manufactured"—written for a purpose other than artistic expression. This was "Philadelphia Baby," a fast number with a repetitive refrain that Charlie wrote, most likely at the urging of someone at Sun who thought Dick Clark and his listeners would jump on it because of the local angle. It bombed.

All of us found Charlie intriguing, partly because he was so reticent. He was due in for a session in early February, and we were sitting around talking about him. Roland Janes, our faithful guitar session man, said, "When I heard him for the first time, I thought he was colored."

Sally said, "I think he could be a great ballad singer, like Brook Benton."

Regina said with a little shiver, "He's so good looking!"

His prematurely gray hair, his soulful blue eyes, and his aura of solid masculinity did indeed make an appealing hunk of man, I reflected, now that she mentioned it.

When he walked in, we told him we'd been talking about him, but we didn't mention the good-looking part. It was fun to tease Charlie, because he was painfully shy. He was a big guy, good enough to get a football scholarship to the University of Arkansas. He had planned to major in music but finished just part of his freshman year. Instead, he had gone into the Air Force, gotten married, had three kids, farmed in West Memphis for a time, and now he was with us.

His wife, Margaret Ann, was his high-school sweetheart and biggest booster. She had come in once with him recently, and I had sat in a booth across from the two of them, having coffee at Taylor's Restaurant. I could sense their closeness and the obvious love and strong bond that united them. When we had finished our coffee, he patted his wife's hand and said, "Come on, let's go, Maggie Jean." A fond nickname, obviously, the way Sam called Sally "Sally Bo," though her name was Sally Jo. Later I said to Charlie, "You two look really married," and he smiled and thanked me. It was Margaret Ann who had brought some tapes of Charlie to Bill Justis, who in turn introduced Charlie's work to Sam.

Sam instantly grasped that Charlie could be of benefit to the company in several ways. He immediately signed him to a songwriting contract, and Charlie also started playing on sessions. Sometimes he would come in and sit at the piano all morning, just noodling, working out some lyrics, a melody, or some interesting harmony. At those times, he would look utterly lost in his thoughts or the music in his head. During the past year, he had written lead sheets for the songs Johnny Cash and some others wrote, a big help to Bill Justis, who up until then had been the only one around the studio writing out the compositions.

For this session, Bill and Sam were both present, one of the few times I'd seen our leader present when they were in the process of cutting a record. Things seemed to be going pretty well. After a time of letting the musicians "mill around," as Jack called it, getting comfortable in the studio, we could tell they were running through a couple of numbers. Then all of a sudden the musicians started filing out of the studio and spilled out onto the sidewalk, headed for coffee next door. I asked one of them why they had stopped so soon. Roland Janes mumbled, "Charlie don't like that song. He says he won't record it."

Sam had come into the session with "Big Man," a number with a spiritual sound that was well suited to Charlie's style. But Charlie objected that calling God "Big Man" was sacrilegious. He came from a devout family in which the parents were gospel singers, and he was religious, having in his younger days aspired to be a preacher. He wanted no part of using God in a commercial song such as "Big Man."

Sam had sent the others on break while he reasoned with Charlie. How could Charlie resist when Sam turned on his oratory? After awhile, they did cut the song but Sam chose not to release it right away. I too had doubts about it because it had breaks in the rhythm that would have made it difficult to dance to. Teenagers mainly bought records to dance to, and I didn't think "Big Man" had what it took to be a hit.

Luther Played the Boogie

During the sessions they had cut last summer, Johnny Cash and the Tennessee Two had cut a novelty number that we all got a kick out of. Whether the public in general would appreciate it was another matter, but in February we put out "Luther Played the Boogie." It was another occasion to poke gentle fun at Cash's lead guitar player, and it had the real Cash sound. When they did the show on stage, the audiences liked it because Luther was even more deadpan than Cash and made a perfect straight man for the star. His appearance, which couldn't help remind one of a scarecrow, was endearingly humorous. When he let himself go, Johnny Cash could be very funny, and the three of them had some chemistry that worked. I thought the record captured this spirit, but even so

I was a little surprised it made it to #8 on the country charts. It never placed in pop.

This was one of the tunes included on the third LP we put out on Cash. This one came out about the same time as the single and was called *Greatest! Johnny Cash*. It was a more attractive package than the other two, but all three currently being offered sold steadily for a long time.

Bad News in Billboard

In a sign that I had been indoctrinated into the entertainment business, I couldn't wait to read the trades the very day each came in, particularly *Billboard*. The mail was delivered by a temperamental postman who was fed up with the lot of us, chiefly because we handed back to him all the packages containing unsolicited demos. Sam had instructed us to mark them "refused" and return them to the poor, heavily laden postman. At one time, Sun had accepted unsolicited demos, but a pile had accumulated with no hopes of ever being sifted through, and it seemed pointless to accept any more.

The postman also resented our unpredictable hours, which were supposed to begin at 8:30 or 9:00 for Regina and me, but sometimes when he came we had gone for coffee. He showed his contempt for us as he would tromp in scowling and leave slamming the door. Regina had explained to me early on that everyone at Sun was a character, even the postman.

One day he brought a *Billboard* I would have liked to skip. There in big headlines was the news of the death of Buddy Holly in a foul-weather plane crash February 3 near Mason City, Iowa. Two other entertainers, the Big Bopper and Ritchie Valens, were also killed. Buddy Holly attracted the same kids who loved our music, and we felt a kinship with him, while saddened by the death of all three. I could see more and more that the travel being a musician required was not glamorous, but instead was dangerous, fatiguing, and onerous to most of them. They were constantly risking their personal, family, and physical lives. The current deaths stimulated talk around the office of the many others who through the years had died in crashes. I guess Sam and Elvis took these stories to heart, because both were very reluctant to fly at that time.

The year before, *Billboard* had also reported that rock 'n' roll had lost one of my favorites, Chuck Willis, "the king of the stroll." He didn't die while traveling, but from peritonitis neglected too long to treat. He wasn't like anyone else, wearing a far-out turban and dancing sinuously to his mellow crooning. I had loved "Betty and Dupree" and "C. C. Rider." The irony of his death and the titles of his last singles was chilling: "Gonna Hang Up My Rock and Roll Shoes" and "What Am I Living For?"

This business was unlike any other I'd known in that we were fans of our competitors' products and wished their artists well when their records came up to standards our industry could be proud of. Likewise, we could be unmercifully critical toward those whose artistic integrity we felt was compromised by producing knock-offs or pure crap. We kept up with what was being put out by the various labels and kept up a running discussion of what we deemed worthy or not.

Sid Manker Makes the News

I had made friends with some of my classmates at Memphis State, though my life was overly busy. I was still enjoying my night-school studies, and one night I gave a ride to the bus stop on Central Avenue to one of the guys in that night's class. As he got out of the car, I said, "I guess we're both going home to study."

But he said, "No, I'm on my way to work." He was on the vice squad, so he was often on call at night. "We have a raid tonight. There's this house we've been watching. Some funny stuff going on there."

The next morning, Regina was bursting to show me the news she had just read in the *Commercial*. "Look, poor Sid Manker has been arrested on a drug charge." The address sounded like the neighborhood my friend had spoken of the night before! We were very fond of Sid and were quite shocked and distressed. It was the first drug raid I'd ever heard of.

Bill Justis knew all about it when he came in. We asked him if he suspected Manker was using drugs, and he said, "Yeah, maybe. He quit drinking, man, and I just wondered why." Bill and his cronies—including Sid, the lovable bassist bear Vernon Drane, and the unintelligibly bop-talking Cliff Acred—were probably as close as Memphis got to hipsters. They called their instruments "axes" and other men "stud" and "girl." I had asked Sid once why he quit the Memphis Academy of Art, and he said his guitar playing got in the way. "I couldn't blow art and blow music at the same time, man," he said. Soon afterwards Bill told us that instead of jail Sid was being sent to a rehab facility in Lexington, Kentucky, for two years. Charlie Rich's wry comment was, "Manker's going to have a lot of time to practice."

New Sales Manager Takes the Reins

Sun had been minus a sales manager since Jud's departure last summer, and Sam didn't seem to be in a hurry to find a new one. But he surprised me early one February morning with a call asking me to come into the office. He said he'd hired a man by the name of Cecil Scaife to take the job of national sales manager and they needed me to provide Cecil with some information before he took off on his first round of calls to our distributors and radio stations. Cecil came to us from Hi Records, a small Memphis label, but he'd worked before that in radio in Helena, Arkansas, his hometown. With his new job, as with Hi, he commuted the sixty-five miles from home to the studio each day.

Helena was one of those Mississippi River towns that had long attracted wandering musicians. Located in the Arkansas Delta, it was important in blues history because Sonny Boy Williamson had made a name for himself as a performer on KFFA Radio's King Biscuit show. It was said to be the first blues radio program. The legendary bluesman Robert Johnson spent some time in Helena, too. More recently, it was the home of someone Cecil knew, Conway Twitty, who had cut some unreleased records for Sun under his real name of Harold Jenkins.

The purpose of Cecil's debut trip was to promote a new Jerry Lee Lewis single, "Big Blon' Baby" and "Lovin' Up a Storm." He was facing an uphill battle promoting the disgraced Jerry Lee. Sam wanted him to hit the usual big cities on the East Coast—New York, Newark, Philadelphia,

Hartford—and then catch Cleveland, Buffalo, and Chicago. After that he might go to Pittsburgh, Detroit, Kansas City, and so on, or maybe Sam would call him back in. Cecil had advised Jerry Lee to get a crew cut and some Ivy League threads so as to cut a cleaner, sleeker figure, but so far Jerry Lee remained Jerry Lee. Still, Cecil had to try to sell this record.

Cecil seemed like a friendly guy, with nice blue eyes. The greatest impression he made on me was that he was large—wide shoulders, large feet, large head, large lips. He was over six feet, I judged, and well built, but a little awkward, like a big dog in a little room. Someone said he had spent some time in Hollywood trying to get into the movies.

We spent most of that Saturday in my office as I typed up a list of contacts in all the major cities he might visit and briefed him on all I knew about them. I gave him the names, addresses, and phone numbers of the distributors, with the names of the managers and promotion people, and any information I had about their methods of operation. Then I made a list of the radio stations in the major cities and the names and phone numbers of any disk jockeys I had been talking with on the phone or that Jud had cultivated. There were also some TV dance hosts in the list for him to check out.

Monday morning when we got in, Regina said she had found a list of distributors and disk jockeys on the reception desk. Cecil had forgotten his list. It wasn't long before he called and I gave him that day's information. Then I mailed a copy to the next city on his itinerary and wished him well on what must have been an unnerving experience, being thrown headlong into such a fast and tangled business.

Cecil was reporting in to Sam, and I assumed all was going well, but it was only a few days until I got a phone call from an angry individual connected with the Alan Freed organization. He dispensed with pleasantries and got right to his question, which he asked in a very belligerent way. "Why is Ceec out there promoting 'Lovin' Up a Storm'? 'Big Blon' Baby' is the record."

I assured him very calmly that we were promoting as the A side the tune that had come out of his organization. He must have been misinformed about Cecil and the B side.

"No, I got the word from some of the big jocks in Cleveland. You have

Sam Phillips call him and straighten him out." That was about the sum of our conversation, and I wondered who in Cleveland had put out the word. I wouldn't think it was Bill Randle, the only one equaling Freed in DJ status. Sam and Jud had great respect for Bill Randle, who had been playing Elvis ever since 1955, while all the other jocks in the big cities were wondering what to do with this weird dude. Jud would sing Bill Randle's praises as not only the most influential hit maker in the business, but the most intelligent disk jockey on the continent. Still, Randle and Freed probably knew somehow what the other was doing, both being real heavyweights in the rock 'n' roll business. Except for my one abortive call to Randle, I have never spoken with him again.

I got both Sam and Cecil on the phone as soon as I could, and they took it from there. I learned then that the Freed organization had a publishing interest in "Big Blon' Baby," and it was sort of a favor to us and Jerry Lee that they had this deal going. Freed was the only big radio person who had stuck by Jerry Lee in the scandal and had continued to play his records. This incident was my only contact with any of Freed's people, but the man who called me sounded like a person accustomed to getting his way, not having his offers refused. Nevertheless, Jerry Lee's record didn't become a hit.

"Mona Lisa" in a New Style

Things began to look up for Sun and PI as Cecil prepared to make his next major foray to promote a new record. This time, it was "Mona Lisa," by our new artist, Carl Mann, who had put one of our records on the charts. Carl Mann was only sixteen when he arrived at Sun, but he had been playing piano with bands around his hometown of Huntingdon, Tennessee, for some time. His particular specialty seemed to be covering popular tunes and giving them a rocking beat, sometimes with a little Latin flavor, too.

It happened that Conway Twitty came in to visit Cecil, who at that time played for him a tape Carl had cut on the Nat King Cole tune, "Mona Lisa." The upshot was that, before long, Conway Twitty had released "Mona Lisa" done in a manner similar to the Carl Mann version

Sun had in the can. Sam had not been eager to release the tune, but when the Twitty record started up the charts, he reconsidered. Cecil took the record to the national DJ convention in Miami in May, and some clever promotion on his part launched the Carl Mann version, which then went to #25 on the *Billboard* charts, topping Conway Twitty's version.

Latest Catastrophe

One cold night in March 1959, I was studying some notes for *Paradise Lost* to prepare for my next night class, and my roommate was busy downstairs in our apartment when I began feeling extremely weak and anxious. It was a sensation I couldn't remember ever before having, but it was so strong that I could do nothing but put my book down, crawl into bed, and pull the covers up to my chin. I wondered if people felt like this when they were about to die or lose their minds. When Sandra came upstairs and into the bedroom, she said I looked pale. She touched my forehead and said I didn't seem to have a fever.

When she asked me what was the matter, I said I was worried about Sam, as if something was terribly wrong with him. Finally I went to sleep and when I woke up the next morning, only a memory of the anguish was there, but I still wondered why I had been so concerned for Sam's well-being.

At 8:30 when I walked through the door at Sun, I saw Sally at her desk. This was unusual. I couldn't remember Sally's ever being there before Regina or me. She often came in with Sam, and that could be anytime from 10:00 a.m. until sometime in late afternoon. When Regina arrived soon afterwards, Sally told us what had happened the night before.

She said that Sam had fired Bill and Jack and that he had threatened to fire Regina, me, and Sally herself. She said he was mad about everybody goofing off. Except for Cecil and Kay, that would have been the whole staff. She said that he had dictated a letter, and she had typed one for Bill and the same one for Jack. When they came in about 11:00, as they always did, these letters would be waiting for them and they would know they had been fired because of "insubordination." Sally usually had a very even disposition, but this time we could tell she was upset.

This shocking incident explained to my satisfaction my anxiety attack of the night before. From our first meeting, Sam and I had often seemed to be on the same wavelength and found it easy to communicate our ideas and feelings to each other by just a word or a look. He was extremely intuitive, almost psychic, and he had remarked to others that he didn't need to explain things to me—just a hint of what he meant would do. I also picked up his moods without anything having been said. This is the first time I had had a sense of Sam at such a distance. He must have been having extreme emotions to take such a drastic move as firing our whole musical staff.

In later days and weeks Bill dropped by the studio once or twice, and Jack kept coming regularly. Regina and I were dying with curiosity to know what had happened, and their stories about the night they got fired didn't exactly jibe. Bill said that it was because he had asked Sam and his friends, who had come to the studio to party, to keep it down because he was working with some musicians on an arrangement for a record he was cutting. Jack had laughed when Bill asked Sam and his friends to be quieter. This is where the "insubordination" factor came in.

Jack's version was a little different. He said it was beginning to snow that night, and he was afraid the bridge between the studio and his home would be closed, as it often was when authorities feared ice forming on the bridge. According to Jack, Cliff Gleaves (a fast-talking, perpetually black-clad Elvis intimate) was talking with Sam in the control room when Jack approached Cliff to tell him they needed to leave. Sam felt something Jack said about "getting out of here" was meant to be disrespectful, not understanding that he meant everyone should leave because of the weather.

I wondered if there may have been two incidents, one with Bill in the studio and then one in the control room. First Sam was asked to leave the studio, and then his conversation was interrupted in the control room. One could see how he might feel his "help" were high-handed. Sam's informality invited us to feel free in expressing ourselves, but it seemed Bill and Jack had misjudged the degree of freedom Sam would tolerate. I am sure they meant no disrespect.

Jack seemed to take losing his job much harder than did Bill. His whole life revolved around music and the work he did at Sun. His friends were the musicians. Regina and I went out to his house after work several times immediately after the incident to let him know we missed him. Jack's former wife, Doris, also visited, and a good thing came of the firing in that they were reunited, remarried, and not long afterwards the parents of baby boy Niles. For some time afterwards Jack tried to get his own label, Summer Records, off the ground, with little success, because he didn't have the type of big artists he had produced at Sun. Eventually, he moved to Nashville, and we didn't see him very much.

Bill kept in touch occasionally and later told us that Sam had approached him about returning, but he was ready to move on. Bill had a band, a family, and some financial security. For a time he was involved with a business in Memphis and then turned to work in Nashville and then in Hollywood involved with scoring movies. Eventually he as well as Jack, who had an interval in Beaumont, Texas, settled permanently in Nashville, and continued his career mainly as a musical arranger there.

The sudden departure of our A&R staff seriously affected the way I thought about my work at Sun. Whereas before I had accepted all the ups and downs as part of the business, I began to wonder how things were going to end. The departures of Cash and Perkins, the descent of Jerry Lee, and now with Jack and Bill no longer cutting sessions, who could predict what would happen to our company?

Sam was often gone to Florida to attend to matters with his radio station there—another all-girl station with call letters WLIZ—and sometimes he would be in Arkansas looking after his zinc mine. Most often he was at 639 Madison overseeing the construction of the new studio and getting it outfitted with all the equipment it would require.

Sam's decision about Jack and Bill didn't seem to make sense, if decision it was and not just a flare-up of anger. I wondered what he had in mind for Sun, and if this seemingly emotional and unplanned firing were grounded in a deeper dissatisfaction with being in the recording business. Even though his untiring enthusiasm about the new building indicated a commitment to Sun, he had had little time for developing new talent and creating records. While he alone had at the company's beginning discovered the artists and led them to find their sound and their niche in the market, Jack and Bill had been doing all the producing of records and auditions of songs and would-be artists ever since I came on the scene. Sam would listen to what Jack and Bill had recorded and make or call for the changes he felt needed, and he alone could decide whether or not to release material. But I couldn't see that he was interested in sitting on the board any more listening to auditions and cutting records.

At this time, a host of cute young teen heartthrobs, such as Ricky Nelson, Fabian, Bobby Vinton, and Bobby Darin, were coming along with a type of watered-down rock 'n' roll. The sizzling sounds of Chuck Berry, Elvis, and Jerry Lee were in competition with tamer, dreamier soft sounds for the teenage dollar. The major labels like RCA, Columbia, and Decca were catching on and began to climb on the teen bandwagon, too. Maybe Sam saw the end, and the incident with Bill and Jack was a sign of frustration. Also, on a more personal level, Jerry Lee's disgrace, following the departure of Cash and others, may have caused Sam to question the point of his efforts in discovering and grooming new talent. So the provocations the night of the firings may have been merely the fuse that set off an explosion waiting to happen.

Feeling unsure now about the situation at Sun, I wondered if I should reconsider my future. I had loved working at Sun and assumed that the company and I would be there indefinitely. I still planned to teach eventually, but had thought it would be wiser to begin at some future date when I wasn't so close to the age of my students. Now I started thinking about colleges that might like to have me on their faculty once I received my MA the next year. The outer changes at Sun and my inner change of focus combined to take away a lot of the magic that had made the past year and a half so memorable.

ARMADA Launched to Shore Up Independents

For almost a year, Sam and some other manufacturers had been involved in planning a meeting with each other and their record distributors to talk about problems confronting the industry. In June, their first convention was held at the Morrison Hotel in Chicago, and *Billboard* reported it as a serious meeting with none of the frivolity associated with some conventions. About seventy manufacturers and a similar number of distributors attended, meeting in sessions to discuss business matters such as establishing an industry-wide return policy and ways to remain viable in the face of greater competition and changing tastes.

Sam was serving as vice-president of the organization, which was called ARMADA (American Record Manufacturers and Distributors Association). Sam and Roy Scott flew back from the ARMADA meeting on Wednesday, June 10, and Roy dropped by the office early in the afternoon.

"How'd it go?" I asked, as he settled in for what might be a long wait for Sam to show up.

"Well, we had a good turnout. I saw some label reps I hadn't met before, as well as the distributors. I was in the background, though. Sam was what it was all about. He got up and made his speech telling everybody how the independents and distributors had to work together to save the business and keep the majors from taking over like they had before. He was like a preacher on the stump. People paid attention all right.

"They gave him a big hand at the end, but Jerry Wexler from Atlantic was sitting right close to Sam, and he turned around and said to Sam where everybody could hear, 'Talk that trash.' Pretty cynical."

Ewart Abner of Vee-Jay had been elected president during the planning session the previous year. Roy said he thought Sam's feelings were hurt a little by not being elected president this year, because he had worked so hard to get folks together. But Sam was pleased that Roy had been appointed legal counsel.

Sam didn't seem let down, instead energized by the meeting when he came bouncing in sometime later. He said the distributors and manufacturers were finally getting the message that if they didn't quit behaving like adversaries they were all going to be gobbled up by the majors. He said there was "gonna be a lotta shakin' goin' on" if certain aspects of the manufacturer-distributor relationship weren't improved.

Then he added to the office in general, "Our distributors love Barbara. That's about the first thing any one of them said to me, how great she was." His face took on a sly look and he continued, "We haven't been selling any records, but Barbara keeps telling them this release is breaking big—that one's a sure winner!" Then he was off on another subject.

Sam was given to these outbursts of praise, but still it felt good when we pleased him. I didn't hear much about ARMADA again, and time would only tell if this association could stem the tide of takeover of the business, again, by the major labels.

Newsman in the Studio

Edwin Howard did entertainment reporting for the *Memphis Press Scimitar*, and I knew him pretty well professionally as well as personally because we had some mutual friends. I was surprised when he showed up one day saying that Sam had agreed to let him make a record to report on what the process was like as well as to explain what Sun was all about and how records were merchandised. He had a light and rather pleasing voice, but was far from professional. He chose as his A side the Woody Guthrie song "More Pretty Girls Than One" and for the B side dashed off an innocuous tune called "Forty 'Leven Times."

The newspaper articles he wrote were more memorable than the record, truth be told. He sold 975 copies and ended up with artist and composer royalties, after a deduction for the $181 session cost and 10 percent promotion cost, with a check for $14.62 for his fifteen hours of studio time and other time he had spent privately writing and practicing.

The headline of his first article proclaimed that Sam had made $2 million with Sun and he didn't even have a desk. The text of the article quoted Sam as saying he didn't need one, because he had four women running the company. In addition to a photo of the front window and a shot of Sam on the board, there was a picture of Regina outside the front door, carrying her huge handbag. Asked why so large, she was quoted as saying, "I'm starting my own label in there." This was a bit of an in-house joke, as it seemed everybody who had ever worked in the company was starting their own label.

MOA Again in Chicago

The first week in April the Music Operators of America were set to convene in Chicago. Sam didn't like to travel, didn't like the crowds, and though we didn't have a booth or a hospitality suite, it fell to me to go and see what I could discover about new trends in the business that might affect us. The independent manufacturers sometimes sort of spied on each other at these meetings, and everybody was "fronting," putting forward the best they had in product or at least talking it up. I planned to go to the meetings, too, and not hang out in the bar as Jud had done. It was also another chance for me to talk with reporters and editors from the major trade papers. *Cashbox* was especially slanted toward the jukebox segment of the industry, but *Billboard* and other papers were represented, too.

Since Jud and I had gone together last year, I knew what to expect and had no trepidation about jumping into the mix on the convention floor, eager to see the exhibits that other record companies, manufacturers of jukeboxes, vendors of technical equipment, and others were showing this year. I wandered around alone the first afternoon, taking it all in. I had been warned not to go to any of the suites, which could be pretty wild. In addition to the drinking and gambling setups, I was told that some manufacturers had call girls for the pleasure of their customers.

In the evening Jack Weiner came to attend the show with me. He was a studio designer and sound engineer who, as a boy whiz of twenty (just two years earlier), had designed the famous Chess studios at 2120 South Michigan Avenue in Chicago. The Chess brothers had been enjoying great success with Chuck Berry, but had also recorded many great African American artists including Muddy Waters. Sam had once leased blues masters to them while they were getting out of the scrap-metal business and into recording in a converted auto-parts factory.

Jack Weiner had been coming to Memphis to advise Sam about the new Sun studios. He looked even younger than he was, but cute. He had a very direct, some would say aggressive, manner, which in Memphis came off as a lack of manners at times. But we got along fine. After he picked me up in the lobby, we headed straight for the bar, because that is where things tended to happen at this convention. We joined Phil and Lennie Chess's party, and I listened as they talked, all the while observing the passing parade. Jack pointed out some of the people I had heard of but had never before seen.

Syd Nathan of King Records in Cincinnati was there. He was one of the grandfathers of the R&B movement, a tough old bird. He had recorded "Sixty Minute Man" and "Work with Me, Annie," two great recordings of my college days that were enough to make him a celebrity in my eyes.

Herman Lubinsky of Savoy in New Jersey, like some other manufacturers, had brought one of his artists to MOA. Big Maybelle caught everyone's eye when she walked onto the floor, truly enormous, in her shimmering electric-blue dress. She was a blues shouter from Jackson, Tennessee, also the hometown of our Carl Perkins.

The evening promised to be exciting, but I soon became alarmed about being alone at the convention. Sometimes with Jack and at other times joining other informal groups, I had drifted from one little cluster of people to another, hearing conversations that to my southern ears were very rude, indicating a lack of respect for a woman's presence. I felt threatened in a way, not just shocked. I didn't think I was a prude or overly sheltered, but I was beginning to feel creeped out.

Lubinsky was the most foul-mouthed of them all. He didn't have a reputation in the business for being a scrupulous person, so perhaps I should have expected to find him repellent. But it wasn't just the language of these record-industry men; they were just so crude that I began to wonder what they thought of me. Maybe they'd never seen a woman in a professional role at these meetings. Surely they didn't think I was a hooker! With Jud, everyone I met had been reasonably polite, now I came to believe only in deference to him, not me.

I remembered the rumors last year about Chicago and organized crime, and my imagination began to kick in. I drew Jack Weiner aside and told him I was going to my room. When he asked, "Why so soon?" I told him I just didn't feel I belonged in this crowd of men. I told him I appreciated his being there with me, but he got around to remarking that he was glad to escort me, but that if one of his clients took a liking to me, he'd back away and let that person "take over." That statement was even more shocking and humiliating.

When I got to my room, I called Jud. I wanted to hear him say my impressions were false, but he didn't. He gave a rueful chuckle on the phone from Memphis that made me want to get away as soon as I could. I booked a flight for early the next morning and waved a relieved goodbye to Chicago.

What Will Sam Say?

I was really scared to go in the next day because I was so embarrassed and was dreading Sam's wrath. Here he'd spent all that money sending me to Chicago and I had left early and had not done a thing! I hid out in my office in the back all morning, but when I finally came to the front, I was startled every time the door opened. In early afternoon, Sam arrived and invited me pleasantly to go over to Mrs. Taylor's with him.

After we ordered our coffee, he leaned forward confidentially and said, "Now, tell me what this is all about. Why are you back so soon?" He said this in a kind, patient manner, and he listened intently until I had finished telling everything about my trip.

I told him about all the unpleasant men and about Jack Weiner's insinuation that I was there for the taking. Sam was not in the least perturbed with me and patiently explained things as he saw them, starting with, "Well, Jack Weiner doesn't know everything." He was sympathetic, not at all angry. I was so grateful I almost cried. I had thought myself pretty savvy, but I hadn't had any experience with men in groups. And these were a very tough lot! That experience told me that, if I ever left Sun, I definitely didn't want to stay in this industry. Sam had a good reputation in the business, I had gleaned from hearing him praised by various people in New York, and now I knew why Mr. Kalcheim had said he wasn't like a lot of other characters in the business.

No Summer Doldrums—Cash Is Hot

The main action in the summer of 1959 was the promotion of our LPs and EPs on Johnny Cash. In fact, Sam declared August "Johnny Cash Month," and gave our distributors discounts on all the package goods on Cash. Sam had authorized me to offer distributors 200 free records with each order of 1,000, and the albums were keeping the pressing plants busy. In one day, I sold 40,000 albums, and re-orders kept coming in. We were still getting strong airplay, especially on country stations.

At Sun, I got used to being berated for late shipments, refusals to take unreasonable return requests, lack of an album on a singer with a hot single, Sam's failure to return a phone call, and any number of other problems. This was a part of my learning to stand up for myself, because I knew Sam expected me to, not for me individually but for his company. It was not a skill I had learned before, since southern ladies were supposed to be sweet and compliant, and also I was an only child so I had missed out on fighting with siblings. Our Cash promotion evoked one of those irate calls.

"B.B., there's a call for you on 61," Regina said. "It's Milton Sinsheimer, and he sounds really mad." Milton, with his brother Joe, ran the Baltimore firm that distributed both the Sun and Phillips International lines. I talked to each of them from time to time, but mostly I talked with their promotion man.

Milton got on the phone, sputtering and yelling, "What are you trying to do to me, woman! Taking advantage of this poor colored boy I've got working for me. You've talked him into ordering 2,000 Johnny Cash LPs at one time." This was the gist of it, with a few curse words thrown in. It was true, I had sold their company 2,000 copies of Sun LP 1245, and we had given him a 400-album bonus. I explained to him that, for a market the size of Baltimore, this wasn't unreasonable. Some distribs would call one day for a couple of thousand and the next day for another thousand. The album was hot! Such a big seller that in September, we extended the promotion. I managed to talk to Milton until he calmed down, and things were OK.

Strange though it may seem, I was more grateful than offended by Milton and some guys like him. His manner meant he took me seriously in my job. I was important enough to be yelled at and negotiated with. I appreciated this aspect of the record business. Chivalry was nice in its place, but what went for respect in other jobs I'd had was actually condescension, as if only a man could talk business.

On one occasion, I had a set-to with our Albany, New York, distributor, Leonard Smith, whom Jud had described in his notes as "keen as a pin." He was an aggressive businessman who, Jud reported, "can get fabulous results out of a 1.2 market." On this occasion, he was looking for some free merchandise that we had no reason to be giving away, unlike the situation with Cash.

He responded angrily when I didn't agree immediately to his request. He just wouldn't let it go, so finally I said I'd take it up with Sam and he could call me back the next day. At the appointed time, Leonard Smith called again. But this time he was cheerful, even when I gave him Sam's answer, which was less than he had asked for, but something of a compromise.

"I'm on the way to the racetrack," he said happily. "Where does Sam Phillips get these women?" The implication was that other record companies didn't have women who worked the way I, and Marion before me, worked. Sam trusted us enough to give us responsibilities greater than most men in business at that time would have done. Our success added to, not detracted from, his own. This was true at WHER and WLIZ just as it was at Sun. Leonard Smith's remark confirmed my observations about the absence of females in the record business, at least in sales and promotion with an independent label.

Not all distributors were difficult, but they were all different. Jack Taylor in Minneapolis was unfailingly pleasant and therefore my favorite, plus he sold a heck of a lot of records. We always compared notes about the weather—my saying it was always sunshiny in Memphis and his reply being it was freezing in Minneapolis. Harry Levin in Boston was aloof; the two partners in New York's Alpha distributorship believed they should deal with Jud or Sam only; Leroy Davidson of Kansas City rarely spoke on the phone, leaving the ordering up to others. I came to know the habits of each distributor, how they promoted and sold our records and, equally important, how reliable they were in paying their bills.

Markets were likewise very diverse. Aside from Los Angeles, we could expect few orders from the western states. Atlanta, Charlotte, and Nashville moved records, but at first I couldn't understand why New Orleans wasn't selling. When I asked Sam, he said, "That's a bastard market." It didn't follow trends, possibly because of having so much local music. Our New Orleans distributor, Joe Caronna, managed Frankie Ford of "Sea

Cruise" fame and tended to push Ace Records of Jackson, Mississippi, more than other labels. The other New Orleans artists like Fats Domino and Little Richard were understandably bigger there than our artists, especially those leaning toward country.

The East Coast and Midwest were our bread and butter, so that's where we had our most important contacts and where Jud and Cecil visited most often. The Great Lakes region was very populous and prosperous with DJs who loved to introduce new records. It was great not just for selling, but also for breaking, records. (Later, the Rock and Roll Hall of Fame was established in Cleveland, partly in tribute to the important role Cleveland played in the '50s music scene.)

Two New Music Staff Members

In the summer and then early in the fall, Sam had hired two new people he was hoping would help to invigorate our business. Ernie Barton, a guitar player and singer originally from Florida, and an Elvis friend named Charles Underwood, had come aboard. Ernie was to do A&R and Charles, who also was a songwriter, was to do mastering and some other technical jobs in the new studio as well as A&R.

Ernie was kind of squirrel-faced, a jolly sort who seemed pretty green. He wrote and recorded a few songs on himself, and brought in his fiancée and lawyer Bobbie Jean to cut a single, too. They were not very successful. Charles was large and languorous. The thing that impressed most people about Charles was his wife Bonnie, who was a somewhat tousled look-alike for the French film star Brigitte Bardot. Bonnie always appeared as if someone had awakened her from a deep sleep and she didn't quite know where she was. Her husband had written a song about her, "Bonnie B," which Jerry Lee eventually recorded. Neither of these turned out to be very successful A&R men, and they didn't stay at Sun too long.

William Morris Agency Comes Calling

By the summer of '59 I thought I had seen everything Sun Records could spring on me, but that was before the big-time agent, Harry Kalcheim, came to town. The usually blasé Sally and Sam Phillips himself were very impressed and excited—that's what was new. Harry Kalcheim was one of the William Morris talent agency's most distinguished members, and one of the few people I ever knew Sam to call "Mister." He had been involved with Elvis since the buyout of the King's contract, and now he was coming to Memphis to audition our up-and-comers, possibly in hopes of finding the next Elvis.

We were hoping he'd find someone, too, because our sales were off, as they were in the whole industry. Singles nationwide had declined in sales over a third during late '58 and early '59. Some people said that with the new Top 40 programming and transistor radios, teenagers no longer needed their own disks—they could hear all the new music on the radio at any time. Also, LPs were making strong inroads, and it seemed musical tastes were about to change again. Jazz, Broadway musical scores, classic pop, and classical albums were all selling in large numbers.

My duty and pleasure for this event was to take Mr. Kalcheim to lunch. I chose the sedate Parkview Hotel dining room. It was elegantly decorated in Wedgwood blue with gleaming polished wood furniture, and the food was always good. Rich Memphians dined and some even lived in this landmark, which overlooked Overton Park.

Elvis had gotten into the movies through the joint efforts of Mr. Kalcheim and Colonel Parker. I knew that story already, but my mention of it led to his telling me how he had landed Frank Sinatra a part in *From Here to Eternity*. Mr. Kalcheim recalled, "Frank came to me and said, 'You know what I'm up against. Get me that part and I'll work for whatever the studio will pay me—day scale if necessary.'" Sinatra's reputation had fallen so low that people could hardly remember that he had once been the hottest singer of the 1940s and a rising movie actor. The public associated him with brawls, his divorce from faithful wife Nancy, his tempestuous romance with Ava Gardner, and reputed Mafia connections. The public weren't buying his records anymore. The role of Maggio in the adaptation of James Jones's bestseller seemed to have been written for Frank, and the studio was persuaded by Kalcheim to give him a chance. Sinatra's performance won him an Academy Award. That honor led to a new recording contract with Capitol and renewed success in not only recordings but in Las Vegas, on TV, and in the movies. And here I was with the man who made it happen!

Back at the studio, Sam was assembling a group of youngsters for Kalcheim to hear. Pre-teen Sherry Crane, the Cliff Thomas Trio, and several other acts were paraded out. The famous agent was courteous and warm to all of them, and to all of us Sun people, but none of the talent seemed promising to him. Later one of the photographs taken that evening found its way into a story in the *Saturday Evening Post,* written by Ren Grevatt and a *Post* editor, Merrill Pollack ("It All Started with Elvis," *Saturday Evening Post,* September 26, 1959).

Ren Grevatt knew the rock 'n' roll world quite well, being a *Billboard* writer on the R&B beat, but Pollack probably didn't. I was surprised and annoyed that the article's tone was clearly condescending toward '50s music and independent record labels. Perhaps slanted toward the *Post's* older readership, it reflected the continued mystification and hostility of the older generation when confronted with rock 'n' roll. The article spoke of rock singers as "musical primitives," with "raucous, untutored voices," production techniques as "technical crudities," and instrumentalists as having "only a passing acquaintance with sound musicianship." Elvis's style was described as "savage," and the rock beat as "monotonous."

I couldn't understand Ren Grevatt's role as the co-writer, because he was continually reviewing rock in enthusiastic terms in his *Billboard* section. Most telling of all, the information was not up to date. He surely would know that the rising stars were far tamer than the pioneers such as Elvis. The charts were now featuring those Philadelphia pretty boys, Fabian and Frankie Avalon, along with Bobby Darin and Paul Anka, who were very smooth and as musically "sound" as the pop stars of earlier years. The instrumentation of the records was changing, too, sparse and raucous guitars giving way to strings, choruses, and lush arrangements.

In 1959, when this piece appeared, the first wave of rock 'n' roll was about over. By leasing masters from independent producers, and luring artists from small labels to theirs, the majors were regaining their dominance. Independents like Sun were really hurting. Some of the greatest stars of early rock 'n' roll were out of the scene. Buddy Holly was dead,

Elvis was in the Army, Chuck Berry was in jail, and Jerry Lee was banned from radio. In essence, rock was going pop, and the top records were coming out of the East Coast, Hollywood, and Nashville.

At that moment, no doubt Colonel Tom Parker was thinking of how he would present Elvis when he came home from the Army next year. We would then see Elvis transformed for his movie career into a smooth, wholesome, middle-class young man that even the older generation could adore.

A Visit with Jerry Lee and Jud

Jud was still plugging on with Jerry Lee. Jud half-believed that Jerry was his own creation, and Jerry concurred, crediting Jud with making him the success he had been. Jerry kept working, despite the meager pay he could now command. Roland Janes was away from the studio often, accompanying Jerry on his live shows. Jud kept trying to figure some angle to bring Jerry back to international prominence. He had gotten two of his hometown friends from the Tri-Cities area of Alabama to invest in "Jerry's future," and he was having a meeting with them, his brother Tom, and Jerry Lee at a beach house on Mobile Bay. It was late August when Jud called and said that Sam had agreed to send me to that meeting to represent Sun.

I made a plane reservation and one for a room at the Battle House Hotel, then decided my end-of-summer beachwear wouldn't do. I had to go shopping at Helen of Memphis, where a stylish saleswoman didn't let me out of her sight until I had charged a black one-piece swimsuit, a white embroidered terry-cloth beach robe, a huge fringed white beach towel, and a chic black-and-white beach bag.

Jud, accompanied by one of his backers and his wife, met me at the plane, and we had dinner. I was dying to know what the big plans were, but nothing specific was mentioned. The next day we gathered at the bay, where they were all staying. A twenty-five-foot cabin cruiser was docked at the pier, and we all piled in for an excursion into the Gulf of Mexico. We did a little non-serious fishing, but mostly just cruised around. Jerry and I sat near one another in the back of the boat, he in swim trunks after he had shed his neat white slacks and dark shirt and I in my fancy new black swimsuit. He was either a very bored or a very chastened individual that day, not the same Jerry Lee I'd seen in the studio. He seemed much older, too.

When we got back to the house, we sat around the kitchen table and Jud laid out the problems he was having in getting Jerry's career going again. He told us all the things that were wrong with the system, how fickle the public was, how fast taste was changing, how unfair it was to single out this poor boy when every other star had embarrassing secrets.

Jud was still angling for a way to get Jerry some favorable press coverage, so that people could know a more favorable human side of the performer. "You just naturally think the worst when you don't know the person. But when you know somebody, you give them more slack." This could be my task, but without a strong new record I doubted I could generate the favorable publicity Jud wanted. It was the proverbial chicken-and-egg cycle, but I had to have something to hang my efforts on.

Privately, Jud worried whether Jerry had the substance to sustain a career. "Jerry Lee Lewis is the most oversold artist in America," he said. The problem was partly that he had never had an act to go along with his hit songs, beyond shaking his golden locks and hurling piano benches across the stage. He had proven this during an ill-fated nightclub date in the New York area he had contracted to do upon his return from England. He could announce a song, but that's as far as he could go. Harry Kalcheim had been there and told me he was totally dismayed by Jerry's performance.

Jud's brother, Tom, seemed to be looking upon the whole scene with a jaundiced eye. He and I had talked from time to time; he told me during a lull when no one was near us that he was a former alcoholic and concerned that both Sam and Jud were headed for the road he had taken. He shook his head, asking me, "How did you get mixed up in this nest of Phillipses?" His words, with the allusion to snakes or wasps, seemed to carry a warning.

When it came time to leave, I was still unsure of my role. I would have liked to help resurrect Jerry's career, but I was no Harry Kalcheim, and neither was Jud. I had nothing substantive to report to Sam, and we kept on as before, trying to sell his records with scant success.

The Rockin' Bandit Comes to Dinner, Almost

Memphis was a beautiful old city, I often observed on my commutes, but at no time more so than in the fall. Giant maples, poplars, oaks, hickory, and other trees turned shades of gold and crimson before dropping their leaves along the broad streets and boulevards of the residential areas. The first frost wouldn't come until October, but after Labor Day the women of Memphis dutifully got out their fall cottons and dark shoes and prepared for a respite from summer's heat.

In the matter of clothes, season meant very little to a new artist I met for the first time in the fall. Unlike most of our guys, he patterned himself after the Nashville country singers and wore cowboy-style clothes with glittering sequins—all year long. He was Ray Smith, a singer from the Midwest who had enjoyed some success with stage shows throughout that area.

But to fit the Sun prototype, Ray was given a rock song to record, "The Rockin' Bandit." Bill Justis had acquired the tune from a thirteen-year-old boy whose father Bill knew, a Mr. Herbert Lichterman, who owned a leather goods factory. When "The Rockin' Bandit" was set for release in September, he arranged a kickoff dinner at a nice restaurant, the Coach House, to honor Ray and the precocious songwriter. Bill Justis, Regina, and I showed up, and we talked and had a drink, waiting for our performer to show. Mr. Lichterman had asked me to relay a verbal invitation to "Mr. Phillips and his wife," a courtesy which elicited a snort from Sam, and he didn't show up with either his wife or Sally.

Finally, the host decided we should begin with the first course, and just before the entrée was served, Ray finally arrived in his sparkling regalia. Mr. Lichterman asked him to sit down and said he would tell the waiter to bring his dinner. Ray said, "I've done eat," and kept standing. He hung around for a while as the rest of us enjoyed the excellent meal. Mr. Lichterman tried to appear gracious and, since I had been the go-between in conveying the invitations, I mumbled an explanation/apology as best I could, but I could see how deflated the Lichtermans were by Sam's absence and Ray's odd behavior.

This incident pointed up one thing to me. The Sun phenomenon and the Memphis establishment of genteel dinners, Cotton Carnival balls, or other urban socializing were foreign to each other. Mainstream Memphis never understood Beale Street, Elvis Presley, and all the other blues, hillbilly, and rock musicians. And vice-versa.

Those Who Didn't Make It

The studio was busy most of the time, not just with the big names, but with an assortment of aspiring musicians who remained in obscurity. For every artist who made it big, Sun had dozens who dreamed of, but never realized, stardom. Some sang country, some rock 'n' roll, some novelty, most all of them a mixture of different types of music.

Two of my favorites were Edwin Bruce and Dickey Lee. Although they were different in their singing and songwriting, and they didn't work together, I always thought of them as a pair because they were our college boys from Memphis State. Dickey even called his band "The Collegiates." We had releases on both of them in 1958, but they sold poorly. Edwin, who had signed with Sun when he was a senior in high school, was the younger and had the more mellow voice. Both had their share of fame later in the music business as singers and songwriters.

Barbara Pittman was one of several women vocalists who recorded for Sun and Phillips International but whose records never caught on. A friend of Elvis's from way back, she was the only one of our few women performers who was decidedly rockabilly. Some of the less charitable musicians complained she couldn't sing, but she was managing to squeak out a living in the music business with club dates.

Young Sherry Crane's "Willie, Willie" and releases by Maggie Wimberly as well as the Miller Sisters were never good sellers. Rockabilly did have a few women successes on other labels, but we were never able to launch one. The public preferred the sweet singers like Patti Page or the country ladies like Patsy Cline.

There were far more men than women who never made it. One day when I was rooting around in the return records, I was intrigued by a name on a Sun label I'd never heard—Rudi Richardson. The A side was a great tune, "Fools Hall of Fame." Rudi was a very smooth black R&B singer who, I later learned, had also recorded for other labels, sometimes as Rudy Richardson. It was a surprise to read of his death in 1958 in the Memphis paper, which said he had worked as a female impersonator in Chicago and had died in a Memphis hotel from alcoholism and an overdose of drugs.

A few of our artists who never got a hit on Sun later did so on other labels. For example, Harold Dorman went with Billy Riley on a label he had formed called Rita Records and got a hit on "Mountain of Love." Johnny Rivers, one of many artists who either couldn't get an audition with Sun or who were turned down, also covered the song.

A couple of the songwriters Regina and I thought were cute and fun was the team of Gerald Nelson and Fred Burch. They would settle in on the sofa between Regina's and Sally's desks and make up rhymes about the people, events, and sights cropping up during the day. On one occasion, they were figuring out a song about Regina and incurred her extreme displeasure when they composed a line rhyming her name, pronounced the British way, with a private part of the anatomy.

They had a few tunes that some of Sun's minor artists picked up on, but they didn't have a hit until "Tragedy." It was recorded by Thomas Wayne, the brother of Johnny Cash's guitar player, Luther Perkins. "Tragedy" was produced by Scotty Moore on the Fernwood label at Slim Wallace's studios. (The tune later became a standard, with sides cut by several artists including Jerry Garcia and the Grateful Dead.)

This was while Jack Clement was still with us, so when Scotty had finished editing the tape of Thomas Wayne's "Tragedy," he brought it over to Jack to have him run it through our echo apparatus. This contributed to the unique Sun sound, and when Sam found out what Jack had done, he was very put out with Jack and definitely let him know about it.

My favorite among the songwriters was the unassuming steel guitar and bass player, Stan Kesler. He uttered one of my favorite quotes from the Sun years, "Nobody won't record my songs but Elvis." People have had worse problems, I thought. The King had recorded his composition

"I Forgot to Remember to Forget" early in his career, but according to Stan, other artists were harder to snare. He was often at Sun as a session musician, so he had a great many opportunities to be with the other musicians. But Cash, Perkins, Clement, Bill Justis, Orbison, and Charlie Rich were all writing for themselves and others, so it was hard for people like Stan to sell their songs. However, he got a couple of covers on the Elvis-recorded tune, so he didn't do too badly. He also made his mark later as a producer of the hit "Wooly Bully" by Sam the Sham and the Pharaohs.

The "New Sounds" column of the September 1959 *Sun-Liners* echoed once again the idea of the "next Elvis." Smooth-talking George Klein, his manager, was touting the Elvis soundalike Jerry McGill, who, I noted in the piece, was "strictly a good-looker." The record "Lovestruck" went nowhere, and Jerry, like his record, just faded out of the Sun scene.

The other release being spotlighted in that issue was a redo of the Elvis debut hit, "Mystery Train." I thought maybe Vernon Taylor's cover might make it, because this was a good arrangement and Taylor had an appealing voice. He had had some regional success with his first release, thanks partly to the energetic promotion of his manager, Don Owens, a DJ with WARL in Arlington, Virginia. I appealed to the jocks to give it some spins, but this was the summer of Paul Anka.

I often identified with these youngsters who came in with such high hopes and felt sad for them when so often they were disappointed. It was a great feeling to let newcomers know their records were selling, and I was always happy if they found eventual success, either with us or elsewhere. I continued to think of them as part of the Sun family, whether they did or not.

My Turn for a Birthday Party

When October 25 and my birthday came around, I still did the shopping for the refreshments, being sure to get the cake with my own hands. I was excited as I opened the small box that held my birthday present, because I thought Regina and Sally had gotten the hint that I would like to have a pair of small gold hoop earrings for pierced ears. Although

I didn't know anyone whose ears were pierced except one elderly rich lady in Corinth, I was fantasizing about having mine done and some day having a collection of "good" jewelry.

Sam was not at all pleased when he saw the earrings. "Why in the world would any woman in her right mind want pierced ears? Do you want to look like a gypsy?"

Sam's unspoken message was that having pierced ears said "cheap." Sam liked classy women. He had bragged that his all-round helper when he founded the company, Marion Keisker, was probably the only woman in Memphis who read the *New Yorker*. His wife Becky was a perfectly groomed, soft-spoken, almost doll-like gentle southern lady. Sam's opinion mattered to me, and I didn't want to offend him. That was a funny thing about Sam—everyone wanted to please him. Whereas I had kept wearing my bobby socks and loafers on cold days, this was different. I put the golden earrings away among my other little treasures and vowed to wear them, but at another place, another time.

"Pretend"—Carl Mann

Carl Mann's follow-up to "Mona Lisa" was the big feature of the Phillips International *Scandal Sheet* in October. The tune was "Pretend," and again he gave a rocking beat to the beautiful ballad Nat "King" Cole had popularized. I saluted Lee Western of KIOA in Des Moines for being one of the first to air the new release. Also mentioned was DJ Don Warnock of Kansas City, who had helped us break "Mona Lisa." Kansas City was a pretty big market that could be influential in getting a record started, but smaller cities in less-populated states like Iowa couldn't do much for national sales. Still, it helped to cultivate jocks in any market, even on 250-watt stations, because they were constantly moving, and often moving up.

The special spotlight column for DJs was occupied by Sam Blessing of KOSI, Denver, who was also trying to get established as a music journalist. As time went on, I kept compiling my DJ list from letters they sent me, from the trade publications, and from distributors. In selecting ones to spotlight, I tried to vary regions of the country and to select jocks who were not in the very top tier of their profession. The biggest guys wouldn't care if they were featured, but I got feedback that the plugs really meant something to the jocks I gave some space to. I think our newsletters were unusual in the industry, where promotion pieces were usually generic and focused on one release the manufacturer was trying to promote. Since radio play was the chief means of kids hearing new releases, efforts to court disk jockeys were never wasted.

Youngsters accounted mainly for Sun's success. In 1956, when Sun was coming into its own, the increasing affluence of the population enabled pre-teens and teens to have more impact on the economy than ever before. Their allowances were larger than in the past, many had part-time jobs, and they liked music as much as their fast food and cars. Above all, they loved to dance. And their numbers were increasing, leaning toward the first wave of baby boomers.

Teens bought virtually all of the single records and the majority of all recordings. When I went with the company in 1958, the seven-inch records that spun at 45 revolutions per minute, called 45s, went for 69 to 99 cents in the record and variety stores in which most were sold. LPs were preferred by adults, and Sam had some doubts whether Sun LPs would sell. The distributors who had had such success with Cash and Perkins singles, however, succeeded in convincing Sam that LPs were essential. Subsequent sales proved them correct. Sun was definitely getting into big business, which is why the majors kept pursuing our artists and we kept trying to get our records played.

Sheet Music, Too

One morning the postman brought a large flat envelope from Grelun Landon at Hill and Range Songs that looked interesting. It turned out to be the first sample of their sheet music that they'd sent me, and it was of Jack Clement's "Katy Too." There was a picture of Johnny Cash on the flashy orange-and-white cover, with a notation "as recorded by Johnny Cash on Sun Records."

Hill and Range had been publishing all the original music that came out of Sun ever since signing away Elvis. Their logo, which was in the lower right-hand corner of the sheet music, showed a cowboy with a backdrop of a mountain range. Hill and Range was cited as the sole selling agent for Jack Clement Music, Inc., which was one of the many subsidiaries of Sun. This was a corporation Sam had set up for Jack to have a slice of the publishing royalties apart from his writer's royalty.

When Jack came in, he grinned when I showed it to him. "Cool, B.B.," he said, adding, "I guess you see that John R. Cash gets half the writer's credits." He might or might not have collaborated in the writing. Often part of the cost of getting a rising star like Cash to record a song was the demand to split royalties. It had been a practice in the music business as long as anyone could remember. When I handed the sheet music to Jack, I told him I was tempted to keep it for myself, and he said, "Go ahead. I've got a lot of others."

On the back of the sheet were listed song folios from "America's Greatest Western and Folk Artists." These collections were made of songs made famous by Elvis, Red Foley, Hank Thompson, Ernest Tubb, Hank Snow, Eddy Arnold, and many other current artists, including Mahalia Jackson, advertised here as "the world's greatest gospel singer." Though their address on Broadway was far from the origins of this music they were selling, it was a major center for the dissemination of the music of the South, where we "folk" lived.

Being Courted by the Philips Corporation

One afternoon when there was not much going on, I looked up to see a serious-looking Roy Scott standing in my door. I invited him in, and he sat down and began to explain that Sam was negotiating with the Philips Corporation to sell them the Phillips International segment of our business. Roy had come to ask me to prepare a presentation brochure for him to take to a meeting with the giant corporation from the Netherlands, which was not only a recording company, but also a manufacturer of electronics equipment. Sam's hope that they'd come to buy his name was coming to pass.

This was a project more easily asked for than delivered. For several good reasons, the Sun "archives" were very sparse. When I came, I was given a sheet of paper with names and phone numbers of our distributors and some cards with names of disk jockeys and/or radio stations. There was a file cabinet, but there were very few newspaper clippings and only a few artist photos provided us by the booking agencies. This was about all I had to work with when I joined the company, and I hadn't accumulated much more by the time Roy Scott asked for the presentation. I had album covers and my newsletters. We had never subscribed to a clipping service, and it had not occurred to me to cut out the ads and little blurbs in the trade papers, though it would have been a good idea. As a promotion person, I probably should have had access to financial information, but I didn't. I had next to nothing, in other words.

One factor contributing to the lack of archival material was Sun's lack of staff and organization. Marion Keisker, when she came with Sam to help establish the business, not only had her job at Sun, she worked full-time and later part-time at WREC television. Then Sally came, but she was busy with bookkeeping and office management, and then Regina Reese came, but by then Sun was hopping with hits and she was kept busy with the phones, processing orders, and many other tasks. I had been there only a short time and hadn't had time to accumulate much. When Roy asked for documentation of the company's history, it was a stunning challenge.

The lack of archives was expressive of the unstructured way Sun operated. Though a perfectionist in the aspect of sound recording and scrupulous in some ways, in other matters Sam wasn't a detail person. Things were always loose at Sun. Everyone else caught that spirit; everything was of the moment or about the future. It took a person like Roy Scott to notice that an important matter, the history of the company, had been overlooked.

I put together what little I could find for Roy's presentation to Philips. Nothing came of the meeting that I knew of; I did know that Phillips International wasn't bought by Philips. I really regretted that the company and/or Roy never returned the scrapbook I had made, because

I had used some photos, clippings, and other materials for which we had
no copies.

Warren Smith and Billy Riley

About midsummer we put out a single on Billy Riley, the perennial sideman. It was "Down by the Riverside," a song everyone knew but with
some newer lyrics. About the same time, we released Warren Smith's
"Sweet, Sweet Girl." Billy's was rock and Warren's was country. I gave
each equal attention, but the Riley number was selling more. Actually,
I liked Warren's just as well. He had a very nice voice. Billy was better known than Warren because of his extensive touring with his Little
Green Men. Also, his record of "Red Hot" had been pretty popular, as
had his earlier novelty record about flying saucers.

Warren was the only musician who ever took out his career frustrations on me. During the period when we were trying to launch his
record, he gave me the evil eye each time our paths crossed. He would
sarcastically call me "Mrs. Riley," and accuse me of denying him the success he deserved. He had had a few other releases, and Sam thought he
was a good singer, but we just couldn't get one of his records to take off.
The reason had to do more with his material than his singing, I thought.
He just didn't have a #1 song.

A New General Manager

Bill Fitzgerald was hired by Sam in late August of 1959 to be our general manager, a position that had not previously existed. I announced
in the September *Sun-Liners* that he was going to be Sam's right-hand
man, charged with supervising activities associated with our move to
the fine new studios, thereby letting Sam return to cutting records. I
had often talked with Bill at Music Sales, where he was manager of our
Memphis distributor, and knew him to be a mild-mannered person who
had known and admired Sam a long time.

As a part owner of Duke Records with a WDIA executive, David

James Madis, whose professional experience had acquainted him with black music, he also knew many of Memphis's black artists. Duke was a serious competitor of Sam's for musicians in the days when Sam was cutting masters to sell to other companies, but the label was sold to Peacock Records of Houston sometime before Bill came to us.

Though Bill knew the world of independent labels from several angles, Sam had not given him much responsibility right away, possibly because things were slow for Sun when he came to us. Thus he had the time to sit around and talk with Regina and me every day. We found him sincere, idealistic, and likable, a good church-going family man. He wore a diamond Masonic ring and swept his blond hair in a sort of swirl over his forehead.

Regina and I decided that in many ways he seemed by our standards to be the most "normal" man we had come across in the Sun environment. He did have one quirk, though. He loved to tear off a little corner of any paper he came across, roll it into a ball, and chew on it. We always knew, "Bill was here," when we saw invoices, memos, etc., with a little corner missing.

He was the one who confided to me one day that in the days before rhythm and blues developed into rock, the term "rock 'n' roll" meant sexual relations. I either already knew or had concluded as much, though in my college years as I was listening to pure R&B, I had taken "rock 'n' roll" to mean to dance, which in the context of many songs it did. Later it meant just to "get on with it" whether that meant traveling or most anything else.

Christmas Party Revisited

Christmas lights started glowing all over Memphis in the earlier and earlier darkness as mid-December arrived. Regina and I started writing the company Christmas cards to our business associates, but we didn't speak of any possible celebration at the studio, remembering last year's episode with the anti-Christmas tree.

So we were not at all prepared for the day we came in to find a fresh, white-flocked Christmas tree standing six feet tall beside the new grand piano that Sam had acquired that year to replace the small upright that had served so long. Bill Fitzgerald was the instigator of the decorations, and he also had planned an office party for Thursday, December 24. We were to draw names among the employees, and he suggested we pitch in to buy one nice present for Sam, which he selected. Sally ordered some cold cuts, sweets, and drinks, and the event turned into a nice little celebration.

Other than the birthday parties, this would be our first staff social event. Everyone else had been ready to start in mid-afternoon of Christmas Eve, but we couldn't begin until Sam arrived, which turned out to be about 5:30. But he came bearing gifts, cute charm bracelets with musical notes for the girls and bottles of liquor for the guys. Roy Scott had drawn my name and gave me a tall gold-colored ornamental glass bottle.

Even though I hadn't drawn his name, I wanted to give Sam a gift and had selected a short lounge coat with black Japanese symbols embossed on white cotton. I got it at an international shop farther out on Union Avenue and thought it very attractive and unique. When Sam unwrapped it, he looked puzzled and asked, with his possum grin, "What is this and what am I supposed to do with it?"

"It's a happi coat! Wear it down for breakfast or put it on when you get out of the pool," I suggested. He looked pretty dubious, but I was later told he had come to like it and wore it year round. Strangely enough, we didn't have any Christmas music, no singing of carols, but we had good cheer and good will to all as we locked up and headed to our homes. I had a dark drive to Corinth, where my mother was glad to see me but disconcerted that I had alcohol on my breath. I had had very little, but she took the opportunity to warn me never to drink and drive.

Tickets to the Dick Clark show, even in rehearsal, were highly prized. On this show, Bill Justis was featured, and I found Chuck Berry's act groovy. *Author's collection.*

Jerry Lee Lewis's first album proved he was the rockingest one of all. *Courtesy of Sun Entertainment Corporation.*

JACK CLEMENT is a name that followers of the music industry associate with the hit songs he has written—Ballad of a Teen-Age Queen and Guess Things Happen That Way (recorded by Johnny Cash); It'll Be Me and Fools Like Me (recorded by Jerry Lee Lewis); and many others.

We predict that JACK CLEMENT will soon be known as a big name among record artists. His new release, THE BLACK-HAIRED MAN, has all the components of a hit record—original material, "finished" arrangement and production, an interesting sound, and a truly talented artist. The flip "Wrong" is a typical Clement tune—simple melody, single message, a very appealing ballad.

Jack's tunes somehow ring "true." They're obviously the product of a basically sincere songwriter. Although his lyrics are not at all sophisticated, they make very good sense; the words, not only the sound, mean something. In spite of a lot of good-natured kidding by his co-workers, Jack has delved seriously into a study of traditional folk ballads as a background for his efforts at creating new stories to be told in up-dated folk style.

Jack's first release on Sun, TEN YEARS, was a ballad. Introduced with a minimum of fanfare, the tune quickly made the "most played" C&W charts.

We know the d. j's and fans who made Ten Years a success will welcome Jack Clement's new release, and we hope those not already acquainted with this rising new artist will take time to hear THE BLACK-HAIRED MAN.

JACK CLEMENT sings

(Sun 311)

THE BLACK-HAIRED MAN

Flyer for Jack Clement's "The Black-Haired Man" touted Jack's folk ballad sympathies. *Courtesy of Sun Entertainment Corporation.*

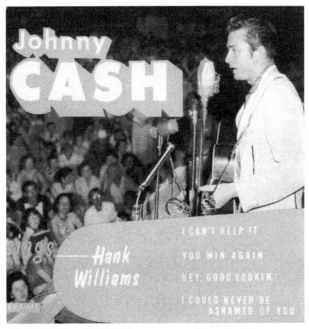

Johnny Cash Sings Hank Williams was one of the singer's most popular EPs issued by Sun. *Courtesy of Sun Entertainment Corporation.*

JOHNNY CASH sings HANK WILLIAMS

• I Can't Help It   • Hey, Good Lookin'   • You Win Again

• I Could Never Be Ashamed of You

Only a few years have elapsed since Hank Williams was living — and singing his heart-touching songs. But already he has been accorded that type of immortality which comes to men who have lived unique and important lives. The little people who enjoyed his music were important to Hank — and this is probably why they in turn idolized this man who was the symbol of all the warmth and sincerity and genuine emotion that country music possesses.

Johnny Cash, whose career with Sun Records has zoomed in recent months, is a singer who makes the same type of appeal which Hank Williams did. Audiences like not only his singing and playing — they like him as a person. They trust him and they sense that Johnny is their friend.

It is very appropriate that Johnny Cash should keep alive the music and memory of Hank Williams through this album. Hank Williams fans are almost sure to be Johnny Cash fans, and vice versa. The numbers recorded here are representative of the best of Hank Williams as a songwriter and the best of Johnny Cash as an artist.

Sun Records very proudly presents "Johnny Cash

Sings Hank Williams"

 Product of SUN RECORDS CO., INC. • Memphis, Tenn.

The Music ♪♪♪
REPORTER

Vol. IV No. 3,—Nashville, Tennessee ● The Music Industry's Most Aggressive Weekly ● Monday, August 10, 1959—AMCE 25¢

SUN SHINES BRIGHT FOR SAM PHILLIPS

The *Music Reporter* paid a visit to Memphis and featured Sam Phillips, *second from left,* and one of our newer artists, Carl Mann, *seated,* in a lead article. Sales manager Cecil Scaife and I form the bookends.

S A M C.
Phillips
International
CORPORATION

706 UNION   MEMPHIS, TENN.

SCANDAL SHEET

BARBARA BARNES, EDITOR

Contributions Welcomed

Bill Justis Disc "Cloud 9" Breaking

OCT. -59
MEMPHIS TENN.

Bill Justis, who gained initial fame with a rock and roll instrumental, "Raunchy" is now making a bid for a big hit with his sweet-sounding "Cloud 9." It has made the local charts in a dozen important markets, and is expected to break big momentarily.

Carl Mann's new release, PRETEND (PI #3546) has meet with instant enthusiasm and is already making its way up charts of the nation. The flip, ROCKIN' LOVE, is a number which Carl himself penned, and some are saying that it's the side slated for hitsville. Either way, Carl Mann has a wow of a follow-up to his smash, MONA LISA. Carl has voice, style, and stability—a combination that is going to make him a year-in, year-out sought after performer. He's getting lots of exposure playing show dates around the country.

Carl formed his band when he was only 14, began playing piano about a year ago. He is 100% committed to a permanent show business career—having attained an enviable status by virtue of his MONA LISA, he's determined to stay there.

New Faces

Phillips International has acquired a new General Manager and several new distributors since the last Scandal Sheet. New manager is Bill Fitzgerald, who was formerly General Manager of Music Sales of Memphis. Sam Phillips anticipates turning over more and more of his duties to Bill —thereby leaving Sam free to spend more time at the control board producing hits.

On the distributor scene, we welcome these newly-appointed representatives of the Phillips International line: Henry Stone, Tru-Tone, Miami; Bill Taylor, Keyline, Minneapolis; Mike Lipton, Cosnat, Cleveland; Charlie Feldman, Ajack, Pittsburgh; and Don, Bud, and "Pappy" Daily at H. W. Daily Distributing, Houston. Distributors appointed sometime back, but not recognized in this column are Garmisa in Chicago and Milwaukee and All-South in New Orleans. Ed Yelowitz keeps in touch from Garmisa and Henry Hildebrand is our boy at All-South.

Ray Brown's WMPS record hop is an innovation for Memphis. Carl Mann makes the scene October 17 ... Wink Martindale's having a big year. First, a nice promotion from WHBQ, Memphis, to KHJ, Hollywood. Then, a TV hop that is rumored to be a contender for a network spot. Next, a new daughter was added to the family, and to climax it all, Wink now has a hit record—DECK OF CARDS on Dot. We're kinda proud of this "hometown boy.". . . .

Comment-Able Items:

Thanx to Marty Lacker, p. d. of WKGN, Knoxville, for listing our tunes consistently on his "happy listening" survey . . . Tommy Weaver, ex-p. d. of WCMA, Corinth, Miss., is announcing at WMC in Memphis, attending Memphis State University working on a degree in psychology . . . Henry Homan and Al Bruce of Lebanon, Pa., are heard on the Al and Henry Show, spinning platters, chatting, etc. Both are vets in the business . . . WDGY's Don Daniel and his bride, the former Rosemary Bialos, are now at home in Minneapolis after a New England honeymoon . . . Special to Don Warnock, who helped us kick off MONA LISA in Kansas City; please note new Mann release featured above . . . Congrats to Steve Blackburn and the new station, WSSM, Wheaton, Md. . . . Thanx to Lee Western, KIOA in Des Moines, for being one of the first to air PRETEND . . . The Redcoats have invaded the Norfolk-Newport News market—in the persons of the WGH d. j.'s who have red remote-coats to wear while broadcasting on-the-spot from their sponsors' establishments.

Sam Blessing
KOSI · Denver

Sam Blessing has a cozy set-up with the people of Denver, having been one of their favorite jocks for nearly five years. At present, he's running his station's Top 40 show. From Los Angeles originally, Sam was assigned to Armed Forces Radio while in the Air Corps in the Philippines, and stayed in commercial radio when he was discharged. He choose Denver for his home because he loves the climate and the mountains.

Sam's hobby is writing—fiction and non-fiction. He admits that he hasn't sold any of his fiction, but his non-fiction articles about music personalities are constantly in demand. He and his wife have one little Blessing—a boy.

The Phillips International *Scandal Sheet* appeared in October 1959 with news of Bill Justis, our new general manager Bill Fitzgerald, and Wink Martindale. *Courtesy of Sun Entertainment Corporation.*

Bill Fitzgerald, general manager of Sun and related enterprises.
Courtesy of the Bill Fitzgerald family.

...DAY,
...2E, 1959

Memphis Press-Scimitar

SECTION B—PAGE 1

Story of Sam Phillips, Memphis' Recording Pioneer

He's Made $2 Million on Disks—Without a Desk

**All in 6 Years:
Gave Memphis
New Industry**

This is the third and final article about one of Memphis' newest and fastest-growing industries — the recording business—by Edwin Howard, Press-Scimitar amusement editor, who got an inside view of the business while making a record himself. The Phillips International recordings — "Forty-Seven Times" and "More Pretty Girls Than One"—went on national release this week.

By EDWIN HOWARD
Press-Scimitar Amusement Editor

Behind the dusty, bent Venetian blinds in a three-desk office at 706 Union stands the man who in six years has brought a brand-new industry to Memphis, and helped make Memphis a leader in that industry. The man is Sam Phillips.

The office is decorated only by a small neon sign...

The Memphis Recording Service's modest sign belied what went on inside. At the door is Regina Reese. On the right, founder Sam Phillips sits at the control board in the studio. At left bottom is Edwin Howard, a one-record Sun artist.

A Memphis reporter called the Sun studio "a hole in the wall completely surrounded by Cadillacs." On this day, though, only one car was a Caddy. *Courtesy of Elvis Presley Enterprises, Inc.*

We had to use a model for the artwork for this Johnny Cash album, but the music was 100 percent authentic. *Courtesy of Sun Entertainment Corporation.*

Dewey Phillips, flanked by two turntables, doing his popular "Red, Hot, and Blue" radio show. *Courtesy of Elvis Presley Enterprises, Inc.*

MAY 1959

Jerry Lee Lewis and Barbara Barnes boat-riding in the Gulf of Mexico. He and Carl Mann were the only two artists with whom I was ever photographed. *Author's collection.*

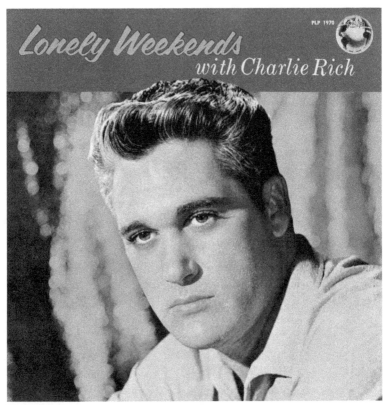

Charlie Rich's *Lonely Weekends* album followed his hit of the same name. *Courtesy of Sun Entertainment Corporation.*

LONELY WEEKENDS *with Charlie Rich*

LONELY WEEKENDS	C, C. RIDER	BREAKUP
SCHOOL DAYS	COME BACK	THAT'S HOW MUCH I LOVE YOU
WHIRLWIND	GONNA BE WAITIN'	REBOUND
STAY	APPLE BLOSSOM TIME	JUANITA

The most frequently recurring criticism of rock and roll is that this type of music has encouraged no-talent singers who have had little to offer the public in the way of musical ability. Whether or not this generalization has any basis in fact — we can say truthfully that in the case of Charlie Rich, the statement is 100% false. Charlie is a triple-threat artist who can be taken seriously as a singer, as a pianist, and as a songwriter.

Charlie began his musical education during his childhood. Though "Rich" does not describe the financial status of Charlie's family — the new singing star was born during the depression on a farm in Arkansas — his parents were eager for him to develop his natural talent, and he began taking piano lessons at the age of seven. At age 14, he began playing piano and sax for a local dance band. He continued with the music lessons until his graduation from high school, after which he entered the Air Force.

Assigned to Special Services, Charlie played in an Air Force band and formed a vocal group which was much in demand not only for engagements on the base, but also at civilian affairs. However, the group split up, and Charlie, upon being discharged, returned to Arkansas. Though he kind of hankered for a career in show business, he listened to the advice of friends and family who urged him to be more practical and stick to something he knew about — farming.

Well — as a farmer Charlie Rich turned out to be a pretty good piano player. He got some bookings in Memphis on the week-ends, and finally moved uptown enough to be heard by a talent scout for Phillips International Records. Though Charlie's medium had been primarily jazz piano with a little change thrown in for variety, the A & R department at Phillips International suggested he try singing some rock and roll.

Charlie's first record turned out amazingly well. It was "Whirlwind" and this number was a big hit in a few scattered markets like St. Louis and Memphis. The first record to climb high in the national charts, however, was "Lonely Weekends," a tune which Charlie penned himself. Two of his other original

rock and roll tunes, "Breakup" and "Rebound," were written especially for and recorded by other artists, but are sung on this album as they've never been sung before.

The originality of Charlie Rich's approach is heard on "School Days," the same old tune you sang when you were a kid — but Charlie's arrangement is so fresh that it sounds like a new song. This type of styling — an interpretation with a bluesy feel — is also noted on "Apple Blossom Time."

Charlie's feeling for the blues, in fact, is phenomenal for a white man. That low-down, earthy feeling is conveyed on "C. C. Rider" and "Juanita," and Charlie Rich's stylings stack up favorably beside the classic recordings of these numbers cut by the late Chuck Willis.

Versatility is characteristic of Rich, and if you don't believe it, listen to the tender ballad, "Stay," another of Charlie's compositions. Then, for contrast, listen to him swing out in a semi-jazz vein, with "Come Back."

Before Charlie went out on his first extensive tour of record hops and TV dance parties, we at Phillips International were a little worried about the reception he would receive. In contrast to some of the current crop of recording idols, Charlie is a man's man type. He's 6'2" and has a muscular, athletic build. He has a firm jawline, ruggedly handsome features, and black hair that is streaked with grey. You might say he's the strong, silent type, but the fact is — he's just plain shy. How were the teen-agers going to like this? We knew everything was cool when a torrent of fan mail came pouring in even before Charlie had completed the tour.

Charlie Rich has laid the foundations for a stable career through years of preparation. He has studied music thoroughly, from the standpoint of a singer and an instrumentalist, a writer and an arranger. He is no flash in the pan. In fact, he's only getting started. We predict that this LP, the first released by Phillips International's Charlie Rich, will become a collector's item as time reveals more and more of the talent of this many-faceted entertainer.

— Barbara Barnes

photo by the webbs, memphis

A PRODUCT OF   PHILLIPS INTERNATIONAL, 639 MADISON AVE., MEMPHIS, TENN.

These liner notes, some of the few I signed, showed my enthusiasm for Charlie's talent. *Courtesy of Sun Entertainment Corporation.*

Who was the star—the Peabody Hotel or Chuck Foster? *Courtesy of Sun Entertainment Corporation.*

Elvis at his most handsome, almost as I saw him that one time in the studio. *Courtesy of Elvis Presley Enterprises, Inc.*

FIVE

1960

Lonely Weekends

CHARLIE RICH (P.I. 3552)

Something to Celebrate in the New Year

Not only a new year, but a new decade was launched on January 1, and it had been with high hopes that, just the day before, we released a new Phillips International disk, "Lonely Weekends" by Charlie Rich. With all our former big stars only a memory, it seemed that Charlie was our best bet for a new major artist and hope for the future of the company.

I liked the record the first time I heard it. In addition to an attention-getting piano and drum intro by Charlie and J. M. Van Eaton, it had a tenor sax interlude by Martin Willis that was different and amusing. The lyrics were good, and Charlie's voice sounded great. I thought the Gene Lowery background singers might have been a little overdone, but all in all, it seemed pretty strong, so I designed and ordered 2,000 copies of a special flyer to be sent to radio and TV stations, the press, and our distributors. Bill and Joy Webb, Charlie, and I scouted around for a pay phone, where Charlie posed as if talking. The caption read, "The Hottest Number in Town," along with the record number. I also hyped the trade papers, and we got good reviews in *Billboard* and *Cashbox*.

Sure enough, the record showed signs of breaking almost as soon as we sent it out. The DJs and distributors I talked with liked "Lonely

Weekends," and not only was I getting pretty substantial initial orders, some repeats were coming in. I was very enthusiastic as I walked into Cecil's office to ask, "When are you going on the road?"

"Well, I don't know if I am," Cecil said, adding that Sam didn't have much faith in the recording. I, on the other hand, thought even the B side was good, another Rich composition called "Everything I Do Is Wrong." Maybe Sam just wanted to keep Charlie in songwriting and session playing, or maybe he didn't want the travel expense. Maybe he just didn't like it, I couldn't say.

Cecil stayed at the studio in the evenings when he was more likely to have time with Sam, so I urged Cecil to get Sam to reconsider. "Look what you did with 'Mona Lisa,'" I told Cecil. "That record was not even in the same class as this Charlie Rich number. This record will hit if you will just get out and give Charlie some exposure. He has the potential to be a big artist."

The next thing I knew, Cecil was on the road with Charlie, most significantly in New York for the Dick Clark show. He also booked him on some TV dance parties and introduced him to some key jocks and distributors in the major markets. The success of the record led to bookings on some top-flight rock tours with other recording artists. All the hoopla didn't agree with Charlie, who suffered from terminal shyness and before long was happily back at the Sharecropper club in Memphis. There people didn't stare at him, and they didn't make him talk. "Lonely Weekends" did indeed hit big, earning a place as one of the top 30 records of 1960.

I was so glad that we had Cecil to promote Charlie, because I felt he was very talented and deserved our support. Cecil didn't have the charisma or connections of Jud Phillips, but I heartily wanted him to succeed in promoting our records, and he was doing well considering the slim number of potential hits. I was able to forgive him for a few little jibes now and then and for representing me on the phone as his "secretary," whenever he needed to have someone hold while he asked me for information. What drove me crazy was his habit of mangling the English language, as when he told a distributor, "If you will do this favor for us, we will be happy to retaliate." I wanted to yell out "reciprocate," but in the interest of peace, I held my tongue, and we got along.

Dinner with Sam

Meanwhile, those gray, soggy January days hung over Memphis, but they couldn't dampen our expectations for celebrating Sam's birthday again this year, plus those of our other January babies, Sally Wilbourn and Bill Fitzgerald. We had enjoyed our cake and sparkling burgundy in the office to celebrate several birthdays in the past year, but wanted to do something special for these three. Regina and I found support for the idea of a dinner at the Embers, a nice steakhouse in East Memphis. Everyone arrived on the appointed evening looking very spiffy—Sam and Bill in coat and tie and Sally in very high heels and a party dress. It was fun seeing them away from the office and enjoying their birthday cards and gifts and the camaraderie of the occasion.

Roy Scott surprised us by bringing someone new. Her name was Lorraine, and apparently she and Roy were seriously involved, because she had just relocated from New York to Memphis. We concluded he had been seeing her there, though as far as anyone knew, Roy was still married. I had never seen Roy so animated, and Lorraine seemed happy and gregarious. She was obviously trying to make a good impression, because she asked me in the powder room if it was OK for women to smoke in public in Memphis.

When we said goodnight after a congenial evening, the consensus was that our celebration was a great success, but the next day Sally told me that Sam was furious with Roy. He objected to his bringing Lorraine. I didn't dare ask why, but it was another example of how unpredictable and inconsistent Sam could be. Regardless, Lorraine was there to stay, and sometime in later years they married. It did seem that the tendency for convoluted love lives that musicians (including some of Sun's) were known for could rub off on people in the business end.

Sam's Personal Quandary

Maybe Sam hated to see Roy get into the same difficult situation he was in. Sam was still dividing his time between his home and Sally's place. Everyone took this fact for granted, and the situation was barely mentioned. One time Sam's decorator, Denise Howard, said Sam's wife, Becky, broached the subject of the triangle and said she had considered separating from Sam, but she felt he was "lost" and that she felt an obligation to stay with him. I had heard vague allusions to a serious psychiatric episode in Sam's past, and perhaps she felt he was again at risk for a major depression or other illness.

Once Becky spoke to me also about the sticky situation, which made me uncomfortable and I could only respond, "I don't know what to say, Becky. Sam seems to need all the people in his life." Apparently, Sam's other family members pressured him about the situation, as Jud had once said he told Sam he should go ahead and marry Sally if that was what he wanted, and get his mind back on his business.

I was thinking of how personally Sam had taken Johnny Cash's leaving and how involved he became in the personalities of all of us who worked there. He often ruminated upon the talents of various staff members, as well as his artists. He noticed and often commented on what we wore, how we looked, whom we associated with, and what we did, in work and otherwise. His observations sometimes flattered and other times chagrined us, but they let us know that we were important to him.

Once while in his cups he was talking about Doug Cowsar, a general handyman for the studio and the radio station, and he was especially commenting on Doug's faithfulness. He said, "After everybody else has left me, after everybody has gone somewhere else, Doug will still be here with me." Other times I heard him say, "Elvis Presley is the only man who ever said to me, 'Thank you, Mr. Phillips, for what you did for me.'"

Putting these hints together, I had concluded that despite his seemingly strong ego and self-sufficiency, Sam had a great need for the people in his life. Regrets, a bit of sorrow as well as some resentment, had accumulated as he saw one person after another, particularly the artists he had nurtured, go on to greener pastures. I knew he missed even the people he'd fired, because he invited Bill Justis back to his old job, and he and Jack Clement reconciled after a time.

Whether he drank because of his genetic inheritance, or to self-medicate depression, or to quell the psychological conflict he felt about his personal life, I couldn't guess. At one time he had confessed to me with great emphasis that his affair with Sally was "wrong! It's wrong!" There was a long pause, and then he added, "But I'm not going to change." He had emphasized on another occasion in talking with me that he loved Sally. But he had little fault to find with Becky, either. Still, his lifestyle was at odds with the religious fervor that had once prompted him to aspire to the ministry. So he was in a dilemma he couldn't bring himself to resolve at that time.

Once or twice, when he had come in sober but obviously affected by a long night of drinking, his black mood was almost palpable. His depression made me feel physically weighed down as well, just being around him. On another occasion when he was far gone, he stared at me and then told the people in the office, "Barbara doesn't like me." Of course, I did like him, but his erratic behavior, especially when he'd consumed a bottle of Scotch, was very disturbing. Sometimes he would ring me up at two or three in the morning, completely smashed and feeling lonely, and ramble on as long as I would stay on the line. One time he showed up happy drunk at my house on a weekend afternoon in his white Cadillac convertible and asked me to take a ride. I told him I would if he would let me drive. I tooled around the Memphis State area, enjoying the sunshine with him, and then headed for his house on South Mendenhall. When I deposited him at his home, he was very docile and Becky said, "Thank you for bringing him home." I waited by the pool while my roommate came to get me, and he was still happy, keeping up his stream of consciousness until I left.

Sam wasn't ever obnoxious in my presence, so his unpredictable actions didn't change the high regard I had for him. Yes, he made me anxious, but I tended to view him more as a mystery than anything else. I think all of us who worked for him found him larger than life, contradictory at times, but admirable in his creativity, his charm, and in all he had accomplished. We appreciated the opportunities he had given us and enjoyed his company most of the time. The seemingly irrational episodes were a puzzlement I couldn't fathom. But we loved Sam.

Daddy-O Dewey

There was greater reason to be concerned about another one of our own, the inimitable Dewey Phillips. One morning as I headed through the studio to my office at nine o'clock, I froze at the sight of shattered glass and blood all over the floor.

"Regina, come look at this. Do you know what has happened?"

She was disturbed, too, and didn't have any idea of what might have caused that bloody scene. I called Sally and asked her if she knew.

She said, "Dewey got drunk and rammed his fist through the glass."

To my next question, she replied, "No, he wasn't hurt too much," but her explanation didn't go far enough. Why had Dewey become violent? No one came forward with an explanation. I had been worrying that something bad might happen at one of these marathon night sessions, but this was the first evidence I'd seen.

The next time he came blasting through the door in the early morning, I had been ruminating about featuring Dewey in the February 1960 issue of *Sun-Liners*.

"Call Sam!" he shouted. "Call Sam! Where's Sam, Shackville?"

Neither Regina nor I answered. Dewey didn't notice, continuing his usual rant.

Looking at me, he demanded, "When are you going to get married? You'd better quit all this running around!" For some reason, I was the only one he chose to pick on, and he asked me the same question every time he came in.

Instead of answering Dewey's question, I countered with my own, "Why haven't I featured you in my newsletter yet? Dewey, I want you to be my DJ spotlight in *Sun-Liners* this month," I said. I realized I had been concentrating on the guys who currently had a large following in the big markets. But Dewey was an important figure in radio, and just now he could use a boost.

Dewey had plummeted from his heights as the preeminent radio personality and then top-rated TV host to a DJ spot on a small station, WHHM, in West Memphis. Dewey, who had been such a trendsetter in R&B and the earliest rock 'n' roll, who had introduced Elvis Presley to the world, now was with a minor country station and appeared to be in poor physical condition. It was hard to tell about his mental state, which had always been manic in the three years I'd been seeing him come by the studio. We had heard Sam was helping him out financially. Sam tended to stick by people in his circle, and he was especially loyal to Dewey because they went back to the very beginning of Sun.

"Dewey, have you had breakfast? Let's go over to Mrs. Taylor's so I can talk with you," I proposed.

Dewey gave a leer across his shoulder as he headed for the door with me, limping on the bad leg he brought back from World War II. Sam said it was the pain from this handicap, plus some bad auto accidents, that had led to Dewey's addiction to pain pills. They compounded, but couldn't fully account for, his wildness. It was part of his act.

As with many, if not most, of the people I met at Sun, Dewey came from my neck of the woods. Adamsville, Tennessee, was not far over the Mississippi line from the farm where I grew up on Shiloh Road. Like all of us, he kept his home ties, vacationing that summer for a couple of weeks at Pickwick, Tennessee, a resort near Adamsville on the Tennessee River. I had taken note of his trip in my recent *Sun-Liners*.

In talking with Dewey that morning, I learned that his first ambition was to be a singer. The teachers at the Memphis Academy of Music, where he enrolled after the war, thought he showed promise as a pop singer. However, he seemed to lack a sense of meter, so they advised him to listen to a lot of "rhythmic music."

To that end, he went looking for records with a strong beat and was steered by a music-store clerk to R&B. He emerged with a stack of singles that inspired in him a love that shaped everything Dewey did afterwards. He became first a record-department DJ-salesman on Main Street and then a radio personality and TV star synonymous with blues, R&B, and rock 'n' roll in Memphis. Before Dewey, no so-called "white" stations in Memphis and few anywhere would play black music. But Dewey's acclaim lasted less than a decade, and now he was burned out. The little piece I subsequently wrote for *Sun-Liners* could not even suggest how important he was in the success of Elvis, Sun, and rock 'n' roll in the South.

Johnny Cash Roundup

In this same issue of *Sun-Liners* (February 1960), I announced the latest Johnny Cash single release, "I Love You Because" backed with "Straight A's in Love." Recording a tune that had already been a hit for at least three other country stars was "scraping the bottom of the barrel" by Sun's usual standards, but the record made it to #20 on the country charts. We were by this time competing with some strong Columbia releases, and Sun's days of hit Cash singles were coming to an end.

Also new on the market was the fifth in our series of EPs of Johnny Cash music, this one called *Home of the Blues*. I gave a rundown on the cover of all of these as well as the three LPs thus far to hit the market. These "package goods" continued to sell well the entire time I was with Sun, even though some of the same songs appeared in more than one album.

The other albums had made a great deal of money, so I convinced Sam that for the fourth one, which chiefly featured songs by Hank Williams, we should go to full color. I demonstrated that it would cost less than a penny more per album to have a cover consistent with what the rest of the industry was putting out. The problem was, we had run out of decent photos of Cash to use for the cover, and we had none in color.

I decided the best thing to do was to use a model to pose for a riverscape to suggest a lonesome guitar picker. One of the young hopefuls who hung around the studio had Johnny's height, black hair, and overall proportions, so Bill and Joy Webb met me one day at sunset and shot this musician. He was posed standing by a barbed-wire fence overlooking a river—I was vague about whether it was a narrow stretch of the Mississippi or the Wolf River. In his brown fringed jacket and holding his guitar, the musician was standing in the foreground with only part of his profile showing, but the emphasis in the shot was a beautiful glowing sunset reflected in the water. When we issued the album it sold just as well as if we had had Cash on the cover, and no one ever asked me if that was Johnny Cash. We left out the Sun logo on the front, putting it on the back instead, and it was the only Cash LP on which I remembered to sign my name. In the liner notes I began, "If there is one man who can fill the void left in the hearts of music lovers by the untimely death of Hank Williams, he is Johnny Cash." I believed this prophecy, and I could see it coming true already.

A Little Miscellany

As the person in the office who was most regularly in touch with the distributors and radio stations, I was aware that there was still interest in our back catalog on Jerry Lee and on Carl Perkins. This new year saw us pushing an EP with "Blue Suede Shoes" and three other Perkins numbers. I also remarked in *Sun-Liners* that Sun would be glad to provide copies of Jerry Lee's LP to any stations that would like to include some of his lesser-known numbers in their programming. Jerry Lee didn't write his own songs and liked doing old favorites like "Good Night Irene," "Jambalaya," and "When the Saints Go Marching In"—all somehow related to his Louisiana roots.

Also in the February issue of the newsletter, I couldn't resist dropping the name of Chet Atkins, who had been in town to visit my former radio-TV prof at the University of Alabama, Gene Plumstead. Gene had left academia to take on programming duties for the Plough, Inc., chain of stations, which included WMPS in Memphis.

Chet Atkins was an endearing sort of gentleman who used to call up Jack Clement from time to time, and I had enjoyed hearing his soft, warm voice on the phone. He seemed very humble, but he could really pick. I had listened to him on WSM from Nashville since I was a child.

I also visited with Gene at his office during that period. He was in the vanguard of the Top 40 movement, which was definitely not a good development for independents like us who depended on introducing new talent. It was a novel concept at the time—management would select 40 records, and the station would play only those, over and over. The individual disk jockey's control and power were virtually eliminated. Chet's label, RCA, and Plough contributed to the demise of the independents and the narrowing of music available to be heard in this country, but at that time I didn't fully appreciate how unfortunate this would be for performers and listeners.

When I had told Gene Plumstead that I was thinking of teaching college English, he thought that was a terrible idea. He said broadcasting was far more satisfying, at least to him, and if I ever left the record business, I should get back into radio or TV. But I was happy with my studies and the prospect of teaching baby boomers when the time was right.

The Big Move

As little shoots of daffodils and crocus were making their first timid forays above ground in Memphis gardens, the big day came when we would move to our new offices. Despite the many problems with a leaking roof, equipment that didn't sound right, and delays in all quarters, the building seemed to be ready in late February when we were told we could pack up all our stuff and move to 639 Madison.

This was a much more comfortable space. Sam had a large, plush office on the third floor with windows overlooking a rooftop patio, a jukebox, and, at last, a big desk of his very own. A wet bar was nearby. Bill Fitzgerald and Sally also had private offices on the third floor. Cecil and I found ourselves on the second floor side by side in spacious rooms with lovely carpet and all new furnishings.

At first Regina was stationed in the reception area on the first floor, but soon she moved upstairs, relieved by a newly hired lady whose main qualification was that she was of late middle age and thus should not prove a distraction to the young musicians or vice-versa. (Sam had once turned down a chance to hire the voluptuous Stella Stevens before she became a movie star because he felt she would be too attractive to the musicians.) However, the new receptionist took a liking to her contemporary, the building construction supervisor, O. T. Being, so far away upstairs we didn't know how that played out. Sam required that Regina and I start alternating Saturday mornings on phone duty, an onerous task, since we'd had our weekends free heretofore. One Saturday morning Sam called and asked, "Who is this?" when I answered "Sun Record Company" in a clipped and frosty voice.

I spit out, "Miss Barnes," as if I hadn't recognized his voice. He got the message, but I still had to work some Saturday mornings. I think he had just called to see if anyone would answer. He also phoned me at home on the only day I can remember ever calling in sick to verify I was really ill.

Except for the foyer and a couple of small spaces, the first floor was devoted to the technical space and equipment needed for making records. The two studios and all that went with them were first-class, utterly up to the minute, and designed to Sam's specifications, with the cooperative efforts of Jack Weiner.

The interior design reflected Sam's flamboyant taste, with shiny golden chandeliers, a starburst clock, fancy door knobs, and nothing subdued. Denise Howard, who was also the decorator for the Holiday Inn chain, searched out these objects and all the non-technical appointments.

A Nostalgic New Beginning

No sooner had we gotten settled in than I began to realize all we had lost. No longer could we all communicate constantly, because we were physically separated. Yes, it was cramped before, but now it felt lonely. The music staff rarely saw the business staff. At the old place, I heard Jack Clement play almost every day. At 706, I knew who was playing on every session and immediately heard the results, but here I had only a vague idea of what was going on musically. In order to do my job in sales effectively, I needed to be very familiar with the music. I wanted to be close to our product, but it was impossible here.

I even missed the songwriters and other folks hanging around trying to sell Sam something. We lost the gossip at Taylor's Restaurant, the plate lunches down the street at the other little restaurant we frequented. The new location, nice as it was, had robbed us of the unique Sun community. Things hadn't been the same since Jack and Bill left, and Jud too, and now the mood changed even more. The best thing about Sun for me had always been its intimacy and the fun, plus the feeling our work really mattered. Now that so many of our artists had left, we didn't have so much to do, either, so overall, working at Sun was not nearly as enjoyable or challenging.

We did gain a new A&R man, the friendly, easy-going guitarist Scotty

Moore, whom I'd met a few times in the past years. He had a sort of surprised look that went with his wide grin, along with a fondness for verbal wordplay. I was eager to hear him talk about what it was like being in Elvis's original band, but he didn't have much to say on that score. He had been with Elvis through his early movie days, but he and Bill Black were let go at some point, and Scotty implied he was through with all that Elvis stuff. I never had the chance to hear him just sit around and play the way Jack Clement and Charlie Rich used to do, and I missed that a lot.

One day I had a nice surprise. Scotty introduced me to D. J. Fontana, who was Elvis's first drummer. He was personable, and Scotty was kidding around with him, for my benefit, telling D.J. the only reason he got the Elvis job was because he had learned about bump-and-grind drumming while working strip clubs in Shreveport. I had heard that it was in Shreveport at the Louisiana Hayride that the phrase, "Elvis has left the building," originated. Someone told me Elvis had to climb out of a bathroom window to escape from the fans clamoring for him after the show, and after he made his getaway, the crowds would be urged to leave with this announcement.

Scotty had brought in D.J. to play for a session Scotty was having with a guitarist named Brad Suggs. Brad must have been feeling nostalgic, too, because an instrumental he cut during that time was dedicated to the old studio and was called "706 Union." Scotty also worked with Billy Riley and his band that summer, cutting some tunes that were meant for an album. Things never came together, and Billy didn't get his album. His band was big on the road, though, playing all over the United States and Canada.

Elvis Is Back

March 4, 1960, was a red letter day in Memphis, because it marked the return from military service of Elvis Presley. Everyone was ecstatic, and there were many fans at the station to welcome him. Seeing him waving from the train where he got off at Buntyn Station, immediately one could see that the rough edges of the rebel in the outlandish outfits had been smoothed to a more polished veneer. Here was a wholesome, mother-

and-country-loving boy even the older generation could adore. Colonel Parker and the William Morris Agency would find him an even more valuable property now than when he had inspired teenagers to riot at his every concert.

Elvis's return inspired me to query a fan magazine about a "coming home to Memphis" story. *TV Radio Mirror* accepted the story, and I wrote it under the byline "Pat Gipson." I did not want my Sun Records identity to be involved with this piece.

Some of the information for the article I gleaned from accounts in the *Memphis Press Scimitar,* which had always had a strong entertainment section. As I said in my article, "Graceland, Presley's $100,000 home in Memphis, was thrown open to the press on Elvis' first night home— and the reporters got a chuckle as Mr. Rock and Roll imitated President Eisenhower" in welcoming the reporters. He stated he had requested to be sent home by ship because of his fear of flying, but "you know how it is in the army. They tell you to fly, you fly." Presley demurred when asked to pose with his teddy bear, saying, "It might look silly for a 25-year-old man home from the service to be playing with dolls."

Other tidbits were contributed by the various friends of Elvis who dropped into the studio. From another friend, perhaps Elvis's former schoolmate George Klein, I learned that, after staying up all night, Elvis awoke on his first day home about noon and asked Alberta Holman, Graceland's cook-maid, to cook him up some bacon, black-eyed peas, and hash browns. I can't recall if it was George or someone else who commented on Elvis's diet, saying, "Elvis likes grease. Every meal, grease—I couldn't eat all that grease." I left this observation out of my article.

Charlie Underwood was still on the scene, and he would drop by with frequent updates as the week of Elvis's homecoming rolled on. He was one of the King's good friends and had contributed to Elvis's image by designing for him the leather guitar-case cover that fans recognized when he pulled out his acoustic guitar.

"What do all you guys do all night?" I asked Charles. It was a half-teasing question, but one Charles took seriously. He thus contributed some insider information for my article.

"Well, at first Elvis wanted to stay at home. So we just hung around Graceland, playing pool and listening to records. Elvis likes to show off his karate lessons. One night he wanted to see some movies, so he rented the Memphian for 1:00 a.m. and we saw *Cash McCall* and *Seven Thieves*." He added, "We might go to the skating rink—he has to rent that out, too."

But since Elvis's retinue is pretty large, I thought, an empty theater or roller rink wouldn't seem lonesome with Charlie, George, and all the others. Charlie enumerated some of that group, all of whom I had met only briefly or not at all: Lamar Fike; Vernon Presley, Elvis's dad, and his new girlfriend, Dee, who had moved from Memphis to be with Vernon during the last months of Elvis's service in Germany; Joe Esposito, a fellow GI from New York City who decided to come home to Memphis with Elvis; Rex Mansfield, a friend from Dresden, Tennessee; Elvis's cousin Gene Smith; and two fellow Memphians, Gary Pepper and Earl Greenwood. Two girls that Elvis had dated—Sun singers Barbara Pittman and Anita Wood—were regulars as well. Marty Lacker's name wasn't mentioned, but I imagined he would be joining them soon. The last I'd heard from him was when he phoned me some months back to say he'd taken a DJ position in Knoxville, which he obviously preferred to being in Germany with Elvis.

Anita had visited Elvis while he was in basic training at Fort Hood, and she had been wearing the friendship ring he gave her when he shipped out overseas. In my article I referred to her as "the girl he left behind," but the insiders said Elvis and she were just friends. Sun had tried to capitalize on the Elvis angle by putting out a record on Anita called "I'll Wait Forever," but it didn't have the musical quality to go with the hype and it went nowhere.

Several of Elvis's friends had taken up residence in Graceland, I was told. Charlie said, "Elvis wants some people to do things with. He just flat doesn't like to be alone, either. It's better having them there at Graceland, you know, because it's hard for him to go out in public. He gets panicky if he sees a crowd coming toward him."

Charles smiled to himself, "But there's one way Elvis won't change. He likes to drive himself." Apparently Elvis had been taking the wheel of

THE NEXT ELVIS

one of his limousines—the white Cadillac or black Lincoln—and sneak-
ing in some shopping trips on Beale Street without the photographers
catching him.

Hearing this, I trotted down to Beale Street to the store where all the
Sun artists, from Elvis ever after, had been getting their threads. I had
heard that Beale Street wasn't a good place for white people to go, but I
figured if the musicians did it, I could too. It was not at all scary, though
I did attract a few stares. The sign for Lansky Brothers was big and easy
to see, but the store was smaller than I thought it would be.

Guy and Bernard Lansky were right there on the floor and greeted me
as heartily as if I'd been a customer myself and were not shy in giving a
narrative of what the civilian Elvis would soon be wearing. "Right now in
the tailor shop we are fitting a group of black Continental casual slacks.
Elvis likes them tight fitting." Bernard added, "He bought our complete
supply of formal dress shirts, an even dozen at $12.95 each. These are
Irish linen, with a tucked front and rows of French lace." To go with
the shirts he bought a dozen pairs of cufflinks in brilliant jewel tones to
match the three satin cummerbunds he chose—red, black, and gold with
lace overlay.

Guy said, "He came in and said he needed some clothes to wear every
day, not stage clothes. This is the look that caught his eye." They were
both profuse in their praise of Elvis, calling him a very nice guy in addition to being a wonderful customer and walking advertisement.

It was apparent in doing the research for my story that everyone
loved to talk about Elvis. They adored him and were proud of any link
that united them to him. From various sources, I also learned that people
liked to give things to Elvis. One told me that Elvis had been seen wearing a black silk Continental suit, as well as a white leather Continental
jacket, gift of a girlfriend who had moved to Memphis from New Orleans to be near Elvis. Her name was Carolyn Frazer, and her mother had
moved with her. Another said that a movie-actor friend, Nick Adams,
had given him the watch he wore. His onyx pinkie ring was from a girlfriend—one whose name was not mentioned. I didn't refer to it in the
article, but I also learned that Elvis had dropped by to see Sam and Becky

at their home on South Mendenhall before leaving to film a movie in Miami.

When the $250 check arrived from the magazine, I again headed for Beale Street. I had seen some pawn shops near Lansky Brothers and I wanted to look for opera glasses. I found a beautiful pair of antique brass ones with mother-of-pearl inlays. They would be perfect for concerts in Ellis Auditorium!

Sessions on Charlie Rich

From March through August of 1960, the sessions I heard most about were the ones with Charlie Rich, for an eventual album. It seemed to be a very slow process and, except for seeing Charlie come and go a few times, I didn't hear much about what they were getting. Finally, in midsummer, Sam told me that I should get some artwork started for an album cover, and late in July I heard the acetate. I was disappointed both in the sound and the choice of material. To me, the old studio had a more intimate and mellow sound. I liked some of the cuts, and I was sure in writing the liner notes to praise the diversity of Charlie's stylings, but I just wasn't impressed with all they had put down. However, one point I did emphasize was a belief in Charlie's destiny as a major star, and this was a wholly honest opinion. I also hoped the album would sell, because we didn't have anyone else to pin our hopes on that I knew of.

Charlie was working in Memphis a great deal during that period, and one morning I was surprised to get a phone call asking me to pick him up and bring him to the studio. "Sure," I said, "Where are you?"

He gave me an address in East Memphis, and I set out to find the place. When I drove up, I saw Charlie standing at the door with a woman I didn't recognize. They seemed to be having the proverbial "fond fare-well." I had heard from Bill Justis that Charlie liked to drink and also that women found him irresistible. Bill said they made all the moves and sometimes practically kidnapped Charlie after the gigs.

It was a little strained when he got in the car and neither of us said anything for a while, except Charlie finally said "thanks." I told him "anytime," but added, "Charlie, when you make it big—and I am sure you are going to make it big—don't forget Margaret Ann. Your success is going to be her success, too." I felt like enough of a friend to say this, and I liked Charlie so very much that I hated to see him mess up.

His only answer was, "Hmmm."

We rode on in silence, and both of us thereafter pretended it never happened.

What Do They Do When They're Not Entertaining?

Charlie Rich, being Bill Justis's protégé, wasn't part of the clique of musicians Jack Clement had built up during his Sun days. Instead of hanging out with them, he spent more time with Bill and sometimes Regina and me. In the early days, this meant lunch or coffee at Mrs. Taylor's. Sometimes it was just Charlie and me, and he also would come talk with me on break when I dropped into the Sharecropper bar. So we became friends, and he introduced me to some of his cronies.

One of these, Burke Cranford, a Memphis radio-station owner, along with some other single friends of Charlie's, kept a garage apartment just for parties. They were young professionals who lived at home with their folks, but had this nice cozy place, where Charlie often stayed after his gigs at the Rivermont Club, the Sharecropper, or wherever.

One Sunday afternoon, Charlie invited me to come to the apartment, and I did, bringing my friend, Alice Norvell. Bruce Reynolds, who was also one of the renters and whom I had dated a few times, was there, along with a couple of other people.

It was nice seeing Charlie relaxed and in his element, enjoying the music he liked with fellow jazz lovers. They played Charlie's favorite, Stan Kenton, for a while. Girl singers were next. Bruce moaned that Morgana King was the voice of his libido; they speculated that Chris Connor was a lesbian, a rotten break for guys. I contributed a Peggy Lee album, knowing Charlie especially liked her. I brought two others among my favorites, *Thelonious Monk Plays Duke Ellington* and *Louis (Armstrong) and the Angels*. When we played Miles Davis's *Kind of Blue* album, Charlie cupped his hands over his mouth and made sounds satirizing Miles's muted trumpet. This was to irritate Bruce, who loved Miles.

Someone put on a new album, *The Genius of Ray Charles.* I was staring at Atlantic's new orange-and-fuchsia label and remarked that I really liked it. Charlie asked me what I liked about it, and I said, "It looks like a pinwheel—I like to see it go round and round."

Charlie's weary reply was, "Well, Barbara, that's childish."

Then I told Charlie a joke I'd just heard, the punch line of which was: "When the astronauts got to heaven they had a big surprise about God: she was colored." Charlie was offended. "Barbara, I didn't think *you* would say something like that." To me the joke was about the traditional stereotypes that excluded women and blacks from serious consideration in religious tradition (as in other parts of life), but to Charlie it was the same lack of reverence that he had perceived in "Big Man." He never forgot his strong, fundamentalist religious background, and I had obviously profaned his image of a God he loved.

Meanwhile, we were listening to the tunes on *The Genius of Ray Charles* over and over. "Let the Good Times Roll" kicked off the album in high spirits, but the mood shifted to blue in several fabulous numbers like "Just for a Thrill" and "Two Years of Torture." With another tune, Charlie wailed along, "Don't let the sun catch you crying, Crying on my front door." Ray Charles and Charlie Rich were soul brothers, both with that authentic gospel sound in their singing and piano playing. Though his parents' white gospel music figured largely, black gospel was there, too, and even more evident in his taste and singing than the white gospel tradition.

When the Ray Charles backing band launched into a swinging version of "Alexander's Ragtime Band," Charlie exclaimed, "Is that Basie's big band!" It wasn't a question but a statement, because most of the sidemen on this album were former or current members of the Count Basie Orchestra, though not identified as such on the release.

Listening to his enthusiasm and his affinity for Ray Charles, who was becoming very commercial at that time, I wondered why we weren't recording Charlie with material like Ray Charles sang. Charlie loved and could sing blues and gospel, and I thought he could be marketed to grown-ups as well as the kiddies we were trying to reach. It might be a chance for Sun to develop in another direction, because it appeared that rock 'n' roll as we had pioneered it was fading.

Charlie Rich's talent was being limited by two factors, seeking to get hits with what was believed to be currently commercial, that is, appealing to teens, and restricting his repertoire largely to tunes published in-house, mostly his own. It didn't seem to occur to Charlie or the individuals who had produced him that a new approach might work. Sam had had such success with blues, I wondered why he didn't get out some of those old tunes of his black artists and try Charlie on them. He apparently thought that scene was over.

Charlie's friend Bruce Reynolds was disappointed in the album we had put out on Charlie, saying the material was weak, especially "School Days." Bruce said, "School days! Everybody hates school. Who wants to hear about school days?" He had a point. Charlie was too nice and pliable, trying to give Bill and Sam what he thought they wanted, instead of asserting his own talent and what he was good at.

PI Jazz

When Sam and I had spoken first in 1957, he had pointed out changing market conditions, including the rise of sales of long-playing albums, especially to adults. The work on Charlie's album was Phillips International's first effort in this respect, though the label had been formed partly with this goal in mind. However, we did have the very successful Johnny Cash albums in our catalog, as well as the one on Carl Perkins and the Jerry Lee Lewis bomb. The shifting audience for LPs was diluting the former teen dominance.

Before he left, Bill Justis had been working with an LP in mind with a jazz group headed by a New York pianist, Graham Forbes. A jazz player and fan himself, Bill had come across Graham in his travels and thought an appealing LP could be made of a trio to include Forbes, his bassist colleague Bill Halfacre, and Memphis drummer Buddy Jett.

Forbes's greatest claim to fame in my eyes is that he had been the accompanist for Frank Sinatra for a time, as well as Martin and Lewis, and now Roy Hamilton. In the past he had played with the CBS staff orchestra and the bands of old-timers Bunny Berigan, Charlie Barnet, and Pee Wee Russell.

Bill cut a group of standards on the trio, such as "Autumn in New York" and "My Romance." I think Sam had even less input in this album than in most of the other singles because he hadn't listened to much jazz. Once when Bill brought in the *My Fair Lady* album with Shelly Manne and Andre Previn, as well as a record player on which we could hear it, Sam shook his head and, laughing, said, "What happened to the melody?" (Irony of ironies—we had no radio or record player in the studio.)

When Sam decided to release the material in an album in 1960, I named the Graham Forbes album *The Martini Set*. The cover showed a martini pitcher and glasses and two cigarettes burning in an ashtray, aiming to suggest cocktail piano. The album title came above the name Graham Forbes, since he wasn't well known outside the music world. Feeling that we could use a change from Andy Anderson's very dated designs, I had another Memphis artist do some sketches for the cover, but Sam balked at paying the man's hundred-dollar fee for cover art. Sam didn't mind yelling at me, especially about money, and this caused another of our spats. I knew he couldn't stay mad because the next day he was laughing and telling people, "I really have to watch out for Barbara when she gets mad at me."

An artist friend of Jack Clement finally did one that suited Sam for forty dollars, but I thought it looked cheap, and the incident reminded me of Jud's saying about Sam, "He will strain at a gnat and swallow a camel." Sam was penny pinching, but in an inconsistent way. He always had enough Cadillacs, even a pink one for Sally.

I couldn't garner any orders to speak of with the distributors, who recognized that the music just couldn't compete with jazz coming out on labels like Verve and Fantasy. Forbes, as a sideman and a leader of Meyer Davis society bands, had neither a unique quality as a soloist nor a recognizable name. The music was nice, but not memorable, and the sound was tinny. The liner notes I wrote were enthusiastic, but my private thoughts had not been. The album died, which I regretted, because I really liked Graham Forbes.

Sam Returns to the Peabody, and Carl Mann Gets an Album

The next attempt to break into a different type of music with an LP was cut in the Skyway of the Peabody Hotel that spring in downtown Memphis, where Sam had once engineered big-band broadcasts. Chuck Foster was popular with Memphians during his two engagements each year at the Peabody, and he had national standing, having played the Academy Awards Ball and other big events. In March, the band cut a bunch of sides live during one of their shows. That LP, designated PLP 1965, was intended not only for national distribution but to be sold to guests at the hotel. This music was pretty formulaic and was exactly of the type Sam had grown to detest when he worked there. Tunes of the vintage of "Oh, You Beautiful Doll" marked the LP as music of decades past.

This time I returned to our old standby artist, Andy Anderson, and he executed a blue cover with pictures of people dancing in the Skyway and a bellman leading the famous Peabody ducks through the lobby for their daily bath. This wasn't a great-selling album either.

On the basis of the success of "Mona Lisa" and the fair sales for "Pretend" last year, Sam got Carl Mann in for some sessions aimed at an LP in late '59 and early 1960. Carl assembled a variety of offerings, and I began work on an album cover. Sam agreed to a two-color printing this time, which made the album a little more uptown than most of our previous covers. I called it *Like, Mann* and I was pleased with the looks of this LP. Unfortunately, when the album came out in March, we didn't have a big single on Carl, and his star shone only briefly at Sun.

I was wishing Sam had gotten into more LPs earlier with material by our established people, letting Johnny Cash do the gospel album he wanted and maybe one on Roy Orbison singing the kind of ballads he was fond of. Sales of these would probably have done better. He had a slew of Billy Riley sides in the can that Sam had promised him to release in an album. Riley had a following that would probably have picked up on this album, too.

My Life Is about to Change

Even though I had not intended to leave Sun and begin teaching so soon, as my May graduation date approached I began thinking perhaps I should apply for a college position for the 1960–61 academic year. Things just didn't seem too promising at Sun. I was taking my last graduate course and reviewing compulsively for my oral exam. I would wake up every morning reciting the chronology of British literature, starting with "Ralph Roister Doister" and going through Chaucer, Shakespeare, Milton, Donne, Swift, Tennyson, Arnold, Joyce, Yeats, Pound, and ending up with Eliot's *The Wasteland*. I did the same for American lit starting with Anne Bradstreet and ending with William Faulkner.

Since we weren't having many releases and hence not selling many records, I used my free time to type some of my school papers at the office. No one except Regina knew that I was going to graduate school. Occasionally, someone would remark about my car being loaded down with books, but they just thought I liked to read. Jack Clement had once advised, "B.B., you had just as soon give up. They're writing books faster than you can read them." Our almost-bald lawyer, Roy Scott, came in one day while I was furiously typing an assignment on Keats and deduced that I was writing a book about life at Sun. He gave a rueful laugh at the thought and added, "When you write about me, just give me some hair."

The day I took my oral exam, the head of the English Department called me to his office to show me an announcement of openings for English teachers at a new school opening in Alexandria, Louisiana. It was to be a branch of Louisiana State University. Since I had worked for a while at KALB-TV in Alexandria right after getting my BA in August 1955 and had friends in the town, these circumstances seemed fortuitous. I sent in my résumé with a letter of application and in June, Dr. Martin Woodin, the dean, phoned and offered me the job. I accepted on the spot. I couldn't believe hiring was this casual, but I later surmised that I was offered the job so readily because his wife was a member of Mortar Board, an honor society for which I had also been selected. It was a nationwide organization that carried some prestige, and I found out about this connection with Dr. Woodin's wife when she later asked me, "You're the one who was in Mortar Board, weren't you?"

My decision was based largely on a desire for greater security. I was uneasy about Sun's future, and at LSU–A I would also have a larger salary, insurance and retirement benefits, and much more scheduled time off. My nine months' salary of $4,800 was a step up, plus now I would be paid to read books!

I dreaded telling Sam, and I wanted to keep working with Charlie Rich until we got his album off the ground. I truly felt sad about leaving my friends at Sun who were still there, as well as the occasional visits by those who had moved on. I wondered since things were so quiet if Sam would try to replace me. I kept my decision to myself until late in the summer.

Another Trip to New York

My Aunt Eleanor was in Corinth in midsummer on her annual visit, and I drove back home to Arlington, Virginia, with her.

As soon as we crossed the Tennessee line just a few miles past our homeplace on Shiloh Road, the land got steeper. We climbed up, up through Tennessee, east from Savannah up to Pulaski, then skirted around Nashville. Cookeville perched at 1,100 feet in the Cumberlands, and Bristol, Tennessee-Virginia, where we stopped for the night, was in the Blue Ridge Mountains. We had come 439 miles northeast and ascended from 440 to 1,700 feet. From Corinth to Nashville, the radio stations played current country music, but the farther east we went, the more old-timey the sounds became. Banjo and fiddle music that had once echoed through the valleys and up the hillsides was now brought to us on radio waves.

What a relief to leave the car at last and step into fresh mountain air, just as the blue-gray haze of twilight wrapped the town in a cozy blanket.

The mountains on all sides seemed gentle, worn down through many years of autumns, winters, springs, and pleasant summers like this one. Here the Cherokee nation had given way to farmers, peddlers, and itinerant preachers, and lately to a stream of cars coming and going through Bristol.

This was the place where, in 1927, a young talent scout, Ralph Peer, had come to town to seek out authentic hillbilly music-makers who could be put on records for his Victor Talking Machine Company. Peer passed up more than a dozen hopefuls, but signed two acts to contracts with the new RCA Victor recording label—the Singing Brakeman Jimmie Rodgers and the Carter Family.

All southerners knew the Carter Family's songs—"Keep on the Sunny Side," "I'm Thinking Tonight of My Blue Eyes," and "Wabash Cannonball." Jimmie Rodgers's blues and train songs, and especially his yodeling, were likewise part of the musical air we breathed. I was thinking, "If there hadn't been RCA and if Ralph Peer hadn't come to Bristol, there wouldn't have been a Johnny Cash, or Elvis Presley, or Sun Records." Peer's legacy would never die, and now RCA even had Elvis.

The second morning of our journey, the Esso gas-station attendant filled up our tank, wiped our windshield, and asked us if we were teachers. "Sort of," my aunt answered. "I used to be, and she's gonna be." I marveled that the transformation I was about to undergo had already begun to show. Maybe we looked intelligent, or poor.

After Bristol, the roads were broader and straighter, right up through Staunton and Blacksburg, then due east into Arlington. My aunt's homey apartment was in a very large complex of identical brick buildings with a warren of apartments. She fed me some good fried chicken and helped me plan an itinerary for my sightseeing in Washington, which was headed by Shakespeare's Globe Theater re-created at the Folger Library. I also found myself gazing at the Impressionists at the National Museum of Art, the dinosaurs at the Smithsonian, other tourists at the White House, and Senate and House members and staff in Congress. I didn't like Washington much, finding its imposing buildings intimidating, its people all busy, abstracted looking as they hurried about with their briefcases.

The greatest thrill was an afternoon concert at the Carter-Barron Amphitheater by Ella Fitzgerald and Oscar Peterson. They jammed, Ella scatted, Oscar brought those tremendous hands down in crashing crescendos and gentle pianissimos. Ella, large as she was, flitted gracefully, waving a handkerchief. The audience cheered, clapping and whistling to bring the musicians back for encores. My aunt and I were among the very few whites scattered through the crowd, and it was the first time I'd been in a large group of middle-class blacks.

One night Don Owens, a DJ from WARL in Arlington and a friend of Jack Clement, invited me to his house for a supper of succulent boiled crabs that someone said had been poached from traps in Chesapeake Bay. He was the manager for one of Sun's young artists, Vernon Taylor. He was an excellent manager, writing out everything Vernon was to do while on tour for the record we had cut for him, including where he had motel reservations, telling him what time his wake-up call should be, and providing pat answers to questions DJs might ask when interviewing him. For example, Vernon was always supposed to compliment other artists' recordings if asked.

On to New York City

After Arlington, I went to Philadelphia to meet Sam Hodge, the owner of the pressing plant, Paramount Record Manufacturing, that we used there. He had promised to give me a ride into New York City, where I had an appointment with the printing plant that was producing our full-color album cover, Charlie Rich's LP. I had begged Sam to spend the money to make this album look first-class as he had done with the last Cash album, and he had agreed.

I went to Philly by train and took a taxi to Sam Hodge's place of business. Mr. Hodge introduced me to his wife, who was a flaming redhead wearing shoes of brightest fuchsia and carrying a purse of the same bold color. They seemed to be an exceptionally devoted couple. As we cruised along in their big Lincoln, he told of the time when his wife had a pregnant lady's craving for watermelon. The nearest watermelon to be had was in Mexico, so he had flown to Mexico City, bought a watermelon, and flown right back to satisfy his wife's craving.

The approach to New York this time was not as dramatic as when I first saw the Big Apple—at night from the air—but it was pretty exciting, driving through the two-mile-long Lincoln Tunnel. The reverberations and the atmosphere felt strange and claustrophobic there under the Hudson River. Soon we came to the toll booth into bright sunlight and the gleaming skyline of midtown Manhattan.

Mr. and Mrs. Hodge dropped me off on the East Side at the Barbizon, which billed itself as "New York's Most Exclusive Hotel Residence for Young Women." I had read about it in the movie magazines—Joan Crawford and Grace Kelly had stayed there in their aspiring-actress days. My room was tiny, but the location at East Sixty-third and Lexington was not too far from the Guggenheim, new in those days and notorious for the swirl of controversy its design by Frank Lloyd Wright had inspired. Seeing it was memorable: walking in gave one the feeling of infinite space. I felt as if I could fly right up and out the top. People grumbled that its walls weren't suited for paintings, but the exultation the building's design inspired made the paintings seem even more alive as you were drawn upward through the various levels of displays.

But work was my chief agenda here. I touched base with a few of our associates, but my most important task was going to the printer to see the Charlie Rich album-cover proofs. The first ones had a weird color separation that made Charlie's face look green, so I asked them to pull another proof. Then another because the colors came out too dark.

I insisted they keep trying, because I had gone to a lot of trouble to get the photograph right, even taking Charlie out on Union Avenue to the fancy Julius Lewis men's store to buy a sport shirt in just the right shade to enhance those sexy blue eyes. We also had made a stop at a beauty salon for a blue rinse in his hair to make the graying look silver, not yellowish. Then Webb Studio had taken extra pains to get some good photos.

The trial proofs for the cover took a couple of days, but finally the printers got it right. Even though the account executive, Kev Devejian, grumbled that I was his toughest customer, he took me to lunch at a restaurant in Little Italy, where we feasted on veal with wonderful pasta. It was definitely not the so-called Italian spaghetti of my childhood! Kev proudly ordered a chilled Pouille-Fuissé, which indeed was perfect with the creamy pasta sauce. The owner of the restaurant came over to visit and at one point asked me if my folks were from "the old country." I was pleased to be taken for Italian, but I had to admit, "No, English, I think." I guess my brown eyes and an olive complexion, plus my summer tan, made me look Mediterranean.

By the time lunch was over and Kev had put me into a taxi for the Barbizon, it had started to rain. My shoes and the marble entrance were both wet. I lost my footing and slid right into the lobby, where an alert doorman quickly picked me up. I thanked him, and he said, "The pleasure is all mine. First time today I've gotten to hold a pretty girl."

Birdland, Count Basie, and Marian McPartland

One evening Graham Forbes came by to take me out. I felt apologetic about the lack of sales of his Phillips International album. He was obviously disappointed. He was thin, reserved, and rather elegant, probably in his mid-forties. He was eager to see that I enjoyed the evening, and I jumped at a chance to visit Birdland.

Count Basie's big band was in full swing at the legendary club. Our chairs were pretty close to the bandstand, and I had a clear view of Count Basie at the piano looking just like his pictures—dapper with a pencil moustache, touching the piano with light accents at times, other times providing a bass rumble to amplify the drums. The brass section stood as a group and blared forth on the fast numbers, and the saxophones sighed as they backed Joe Williams's ballads.

This singer was a marvel. A tall dark man in a fine-looking suit, Williams opened his mouth wide and the sound just rolled out. No straining for high or low notes, no contorted facial expressions, just beautiful warm sound. He didn't move much when he sang, but every word expressed an emotion, as in "Every Day I Have the Blues" or "Please Send Me Someone to Love."

When the band finished its set, we didn't want the music to end, so Graham steered me over a few blocks to another part of Fifty-second Street to the Hickory House. The club was dimly lit, and people were having dinner. Here the music was more atmospheric, not the main attraction for which you sat on the edge of your chairs. But there was a grand piano presided over by Marian McPartland, accompanied by her bass player and drummer. They were playing some very nice jazz, which we listened to while having a nightcap.

I told Graham that I had framed his Christmas card of the previous year, a lovely Madonna and Child. He promised to have his daughter do me a chalk drawing of the BVM (as he expressed it), and not long after I returned to Memphis, his daughter's pretty drawing came in the mail.

Josh White at Ravinia Festival

Instead of flying back directly to Memphis from New York, I caught a plane for Chicago to visit friends. This flight across half the country was another new experience for me, and it was exciting as we neared Chicago to see Lake Michigan glittering in the sunlight. It seemed to go on and on—I understood at last why Lake Michigan and its companions were called the Great Lakes. During the ride from the airport to my friends' house, I heard Dick Biondi announce on WLS, "Barbara Barnes is in town this weekend and here's a song just for her, 'Itsy Bitsy Teenie Weenie Yellow Polka Dot Bikini.'" I had told him I was coming, but it was pure coincidence that I heard the dedication in the taxi.

I was glad to see Jackie and Dick Chaussee again, and this time it was their turn to entertain me. I had some time before acquired an LP of Josh White's, and it was thrilling to see him in person at the Ravinia Festival in Highland Park on the North Shore of Lake Michigan. This guitar-playing singer was ahead of the soon-to-come folk trend, blending a repertoire of traditional songs like "Molly Malone" with bluesy guitar accompaniment. In his urbanity, he was unlike the black entertainers I had seen in the South, but he too was southern, from South Carolina.

I had read he played in Europe often and was the darling of posh New

York café society. A friend who had seen him in a San Francisco club had described him as very sexy and arrogant, propping his foot on a chair and looking at the audience as if to say any woman here was his for the taking. He could do a tender "Call Me Darling" or a raunchy "I'm Gonna Move You Way on the Outskirts of Town." We had to sit on the ground to hear him, but even outdoors and some distance away, you had to know that Josh White was a star and one you would never forget.

Back Home

When I got back, I tried to convince Billy Riley to develop a single act modeled after Josh White. Billy was really good looking, and when he wasn't shouting as he did on his rock records, he had a passable voice. He played guitar well, and I thought the time was right for some blues and folk music. I knew he'd grown up alongside black workers in the cotton fields of Arkansas and that he knew all kinds of blues songs. I saw him as a Josh White, just a little lighter with his olive complexion and glossy black hair.

"Why don't you see if you can get a solo booking at the Rivermont? You could wear a black turtleneck and pants and get close to your audience. You could really sing to them, instead of shouting and jumping around. The ladies will love you if you'll romance them a little. You could try out some material that way and find some blues to record."

"Yeah," he crooned. "Sex-ville." No one at Sun was thinking of selling folk-based records, but I thought it could be done. Billy listened to me thoughtfully, his eyes lighting up, and I could see he was envisioning himself as a cabaret singer. This new musical identity would allow him to re-invent himself. He was always saying his name was unlucky, and if he could just find the right name, he was sure he'd be a star. With other labels later, he recorded as Darren Lee and Skip Wylie before finally settling on adding Lee to his name, thereby coming to be remembered as Billy Lee Riley.

He didn't follow up on my advice for a single act, but he did put his blues roots out there when he formed his own label, Rita Records, sometime later. Calling himself "Lightnin' Leon," he sounded like an authentic blues singer on a tune called "Repossession Blues." The back side, all about the endless hours farm laborers spent in those times driving a mule down cotton furrows, was also authentic-sounding blues. He was a fine harmonica player and, as one whose family were the only white sharecroppers on a large Arkansas plantation, he came as close as a white man could come to playing the real Delta blues.

I Finally Tell Sam

As August came along with its long, sweltering days, I knew I had to face the task of telling Sam I was leaving. I appreciated him more than any boss I'd ever had for many reasons, most important for his unique, generous, maddening, ever-changing self and for the benefits I had received working for him. Observing and listening to Sam had taught me a great deal, and I felt I had grown personally and professionally in my days at Sun.

I went down one evening and found him in the old studio. No one else was in the reception area, and we sat down together on the little green loveseat. I told him I was leaving, and he asked what I was going to do. He didn't express surprise that I was qualified to teach in college, and he didn't try to convince me to reconsider. He simply congratulated me and said, "You can always have a job with me. Even if this record business doesn't pick up, I'll always have other places you can fit in." He couldn't have been more gracious.

Later when the word got out that I was leaving, Denise Howard reported a conversation she had with Sam about my resignation. Sam said, according to Denise, "This business is just a little too crazy for Barbara." I appreciated his sensitivity and understanding, and he had read me right, as he did with almost everyone else.

My last day at work was a Friday, and I packed up my little box of things and drove away from the studio with mixed feelings. I was excited to be going to my new life as a college teacher, but I knew I was leaving a unique phase of my life. Denise Howard had once said, "You don't work for Sam Phillips without it changing you." That was true, but there was something else: I knew most deeply that I would never again work where

I could truly be myself and express myself, my whole person, with the degree of freedom I had had at Sun. Observing my fellow employees and myself, I had come to believe that, with Sam, you found out who you truly were, because you were on your own. You were there to do what you *could* do, and he was standing back to see what you *would* do. He tolerated a good bit of aberrant behavior, but I had found that the laissez-faire atmosphere had made me more, not less, responsible and able to be more effective than in other jobs where there was no room for creativity.

With his company employees, he followed the same philosophy and practiced the same alchemy he used to get the best, the authentic self, out of Elvis, Johnny, Jerry Lee, and Carl. In fact, I reflected that I owed Sam Phillips the greatest debt of my life. He gave me to myself. He was my final father figure, who convinced me of my ability to meet the challenges of my life capably. During this time I also came to know that I didn't always have to be unduly concerned about anyone else's approval. I had proven to myself that I was able to guide my own actions and decisions. My horizons had been broadened, and I had been freed of some of my small-town judgmental attitudes. He had taught me by example to be more imaginative about the possibilities each person might possess.

A Night to Remember

The next day I packed up my '59 Chevy (I had some newer wheels by then), and that evening, I had a date with Jim Price, a TV producer I had kept in touch with since our days at WMCT. I was surprised when he said he wanted to stop by Sun, because he had an appointment to talk with Sam about applying for my job. On Saturday night? How insensitive, I thought. To think he could take *my* place.

When we arrived, there they all were—the Sun gang. They had organized a rooftop going-away party for me. On that early summer evening, the sun was just setting over the Mississippi River to the west. Out east, the lights were beginning to come on along the major streets—Poplar, Madison, Union. This beautiful evening and the festive atmosphere on that open-air patio made me feel terribly nostalgic about Memphis even while I was still there. How different it was from the vacant feeling when I had looked down from the Peabody roof three years before and heard a new friend tell me that there was nothing out there. I had found unforgettable people, music, and experiences just a few blocks away at 706 Union.

At the party the guests found a bar, fried chicken, and other catered southern delicacies, and music on the stereo. Margaret Ann and Charlie Rich were there and had brought me an elegant blue rhinestone earring-and-pin set. Scotty Moore, Bill, Cecil, Regina, Sally, Sam, Roy, and Denise were there, too. Some others may have drifted in. I had my share of scotch and soda that night. I recall kissing Charlie and Scotty goodbye, maybe several times, and heaven knows who else. It was a nice send-off.

A New Adventure

Very early on the morning following my going-away party, I set off down Highway 61 towards the Mississippi Delta. I was going on the same road, but in the opposite direction, that had brought B.B. King, Little Junior Parker, Ike Turner, and so many other great bluesmen to Memphis. Riding along with me on the radio was one of the black gospel groups like the Jolly Sunshine Boosters that I had loved so much when I was a small child. Their spirituals always seemed like Sunday to me. On that morning in 1960, as on each Sunday morning, programming was given over to religious music or church services. When the signal from one small town's station faded, I would find another, picking up gospel quartets and white and black preachers. One of the latter was singing his sermon, and the worshippers were responding to his exhortations, sometimes repeating what he had said, sometimes shouting "that's right" or "amen."

I thought of Sam and Carl, Elvis, Johnny, Jerry Lee, and Charlie—all with this music in their bones.

Near Greenville I needed to buy gas, so I pulled into an Esso station and filled up my Chevy. Then I got an unpleasant surprise. When I opened my wallet to pay for the gas and a Coke, I found someone at my going-away party had stolen the forty dollars of travel money I had withdrawn from the bank. What an ironic anti-climax to such a great party! Luckily, I had an Esso credit card.

As I started out again, crossing the high bridge that spans the Mississippi River and leads west into Arkansas, I tuned into a live broadcast from the Methodist church. The choir was singing "Amazing Grace," and a few lines of the hymn seemed meant for me:

> Through many dangers, toils and snares
> I have already come
> 'Tis grace hath brought me safe thus far,
> And grace will lead me home.

When I turned south again toward Bastrop, Monroe, and my new home in Alexandria, Louisiana, I was thinking that the party and the theft were a fitting end to the Sun chapter of my life. What apt symbols of the wonderful, memorable surprises and disappointing turns of fate that those three years held. At Memphis State I was taught that a drama requires a significant theme, along with enough conflict and tension to make an interesting story. At Sun, I had witnessed three years of pure drama played out before my eyes. It was a small studio—706 Union Avenue, Memphis, Tennessee—but such a big chunk of life! Sherwood Anderson, one of my favorite writers, said that for him writing was "love in words." At Sun, making music was "love in sound." That love has echoed in my heart and mind wherever I've gone, all the days of my life.

EPILOGUE

SUN RECORD COMPANY AND PHILLIPS INTERNATIONAL continued in business until 1968, when Sam Phillips sold their catalogs to Shelby Singleton, a Nashville producer. Singleton re-launched the company as Sun International Corporation and subsequently packaged, re-released, and licensed the recordings to companies for re-issue and for box sets. These releases brought Sun's music to even wider audiences, which led to greater appreciation of Sam Phillips's early work with black artists from Memphis and the Mississippi and Arkansas deltas. Later the company was re-named Sun Entertainment Corporation, and it continues today with offices in Nashville, although Shelby Singleton is now deceased.

Sun has the most instantly recognizable record label in existence, the yellow circle of the sun with fourteen sun rays, centered with a crowing rooster. The original studio and the adjacent café, formerly Mrs. Taylor's restaurant, have been converted into one space that has been accorded National Historic Register recognition. Sun Studios, not related to the original company, offers tours during which visitors may see the exact spot Elvis stood while recording, equipment from the studio, and pictures and other memorabilia in the studio and on the second story of the restaurant.

BARBARA BARNES SIMS (1933–) taught English at LSU–Alexandria for three years immediately after leaving Sun, during which time she married Robert Sims and they had a daughter, Sue Sims. In 1963 they moved to Baton Rouge, where she taught in the Department of English at Louisiana State University until retiring in 1996. She was honored with two major university-wide teaching awards, and a scholarship was named in her honor. She edited several alumni publications at LSU, as well as publishing freelance feature articles and scholarly papers on music, literature, folklore, and pedagogy. After leaving LSU, she became an independent technical and business writing consultant for the State of Louisiana and major industrial corporations. Her husband passed away in 2004, and her daughter resides in Kentucky at a home for individuals with special needs. Barbara lectures on rock 'n' roll and literature at continuing-education classes at Chautauqua Institution in New York State, at university adult-education classes, and for several cruise lines.

EDWIN BRUCE (1933–) lives in Nashville, where he is known as Ed Bruce, the writer of many hit country songs, including the smash hit "Mamas, Don't Let Your Babies Grow Up to Be Cowboys," sung by Willie Nelson and Waylon Jennings. He co-starred in the TV series *Maverick* and has acted in many films. He is retired from show business and now gives inspirational talks to Christian audiences and also trains dogs.

JOHNNY CASH (1932–2003). The honors Cash received—membership in the Country Music, Rock and Roll, Rockabilly, and Songwriters Halls of Fame, among many others—attest to the quality and versatility of Cash's long career. He was presented the Grammy Lifetime Achievement Award and various individual Grammys and received Kennedy Center Honors. In addition to his singing and playing, he performed as an actor and as a network TV host, where he was termed "The Man in Black." The movie *Walk the Line* was a partially fictionalized story of his life, emphasizing his marriage to June Carter and their musical collaboration.

JACK CLEMENT (1931–2013) became a Nashville legend as a songwriter, producer, singer/guitarist/ bandleader, radio host, and all-around character. After leaving Sun, he discovered and produced Charley Pride and recorded numerous entertainers, including Waylon Jennings, Don Williams, U2, and his good friend Johnny Cash. His many original songs have been recorded by everyone from Dolly Parton to Ray Charles. He is a member of the Nashville Songwriters Hall of Fame, the Country Music Hall of Fame, and the Rockabilly Hall of Fame. He released two CDs on himself, on one of which Johnny Cash sang back-up on some numbers.

During a time when he maintained a studio in Beaumont, Texas, he acquired the nickname "Cowboy."

BILL FITZGERALD (1920–1991) remained with Sun until 1969, when he took a position with a major recording label in Nashville, serving in A&R management until his retirement.

CLIFF GLEAVES (1930–2002) remained a sometime member of the Memphis Mafia.

ROLAND JANES (1933–2013) continued playing with the bands of Jerry Lee Lewis and Billy Riley until he retired to be in charge of Phillips Recording Service in Memphis, where he was employed until shortly before his death.

BILL JUSTIS (1926–1982), after leaving Sun, worked both in Hollywood and Nashville, where he was sought after as an A&R man, producer, arranger, performer, and session player. He composed the music for several well-known movies, including *Smokey and the Bandit*.

GEORGE KLEIN (1935–) hosts two Sirius radio programs devoted to Elvis music and participates in Elvis commemorative events. He has been employed with a casino in the Memphis area.

MARTY LACKER (1936–) joined the Elvis Presley entourage and was co–best man at Elvis's wedding to Priscilla Wagner. He was with Elvis for twenty years, serving as "foreman" of the group that was charged with "taking care of business."

JERRY LEE LEWIS (1935–), in an album released in 2006, is referred to as "The Last Man Standing." This is a reference to his being the last surviving member of the Million Dollar Quartet. This group (Elvis, Carl, Johnny, and Jerry Lee) and an episode in their lives at Sun with Sam Phillips have been depicted in the Broadway musical *Million Dollar Quartet*. Jerry Lee Lewis's recording career was revived in the 1970s with a succession of hit country singles and several albums. A member of the Rock and Roll Hall of Fame, he was honored at a special tribute concert there in 2007, and his contribution to rock music was the subject of a five-day conference that year at Case Western Reserve University. He is recognized among rock aficionados as the personification of what he has said is "the devil's music." He still makes occasional TV and personal appearances. He lives in Mississippi in a suburb of Memphis. Jerry Lee and Myra were married for twelve years before being divorced. Since that time he has had six additional wives, one at a time, of whom he was divorced from three. Two predeceased him.

DICKEY LEE (1936–) lives in Nashville and is known as the composer of many classic country songs, including the country standard "She Thinks I Still Care." He also made top-selling records in the 1960s and is still singing, including for charitable organizations.

SID MANKER (1932–1974) continued to "blow jazz" until his death in Biloxi, Mississippi. When George Harrison auditioned for the Beatles, he played Sid's "Raunchy" solo to gain a spot in the Fab Four.

WINK MARTINDALE (1934–) felt the lure of Hollywood, where he became a popular DJ and later host of several national TV game shows. He was honored with a star on the Hollywood Walk of Fame in 2006.

SCOTTY MOORE (1931–) established a custom recording studio in Nashville upon leaving Sun and continued to play with Elvis Presley and others on occasion. *Rolling Stone* ranked him #29 of the greatest 100 guitarists of all time, and he has been credited for establishing the importance of the lead guitar in rock bands. The Gibson guitar company named one of its products the "Scotty Moore Guitar."

ROY ORBISON (1936–1988) established himself as a premier figure in rock music by recording a series of hit songs, many that he himself composed. He was especially popular in Europe and made his home there for a number of years. His song "Pretty Woman" charted at #1 in many countries around the globe and was the title song of a major movie. He was able to enhance his popularity when British rock threatened to obscure rockabilly by performing with the Beatles and the Rolling Stones. He was a part of a supergroup called the Traveling Wilburys in the 1980s with Bob Dylan, George Harrison, and Jeff Lynne. He is a Grammy-winning member of the Rock and Roll and Songwriters Halls of Fame.

CARL PERKINS (1932–1998) languished in musical limbo for a time after his initial success at Sun. However, his musical career was revived in the 1960s when the Beatles recorded several of his tunes and the Rolling Stones invited him to open for them. John Lennon spoke of him as his favorite musician. He was inducted into the Rock and Roll, Nashville Songwriters, and the Rockabilly Halls of Fame and received the Grammy Hall of Fame honor as well.

DEWEY PHILLIPS (1926–1968) is a name that will forever be linked to that of Elvis Presley. The Broadway musical *Memphis* was loosely based on Dewey's time as an inimitable early rock DJ.

JUD PHILLIPS (1921–1992) continued to manage Jerry Lee Lewis after he left Sun and until his retirement. Informed rock critics have termed him the "father of the modern record promoter." For a time he and Sam, along with their sons, reunited and formed Holiday Inn Records, but the label was short-lived.

SAM PHILLIPS (1923–2003), along with two of his discoveries, Elvis Presley and Jerry Lee Lewis, was included in the first group of rock 'n' roll pioneers inducted into the Rock and Roll Hall of Fame. Sam was also inducted into the Country Music Hall of Fame, the Rockabilly Hall of Fame, the Alabama Music Hall of Fame, the Blues Foundation Hall of Fame, and the TEC Awards Hall of Fame for excellence and creativity in the recording industry. He is the only person accorded the distinction of membership in all of these honor rolls of music.

In the 1960s he became increasingly involved with the group of radio stations he had acquired, finally leaving the record business after 1968, when he sold the Sun catalog. At that time, he said, "But by God, I didn't sell to the majors." His pessimistic prophecy concerning the future of independent labels was fulfilled, because by the time of his death most of them had been sold to the major labels or had gone out of business.

At his death, he was survived by his wife, Becky Phillips; two sons, Knox and Jerry Phillips; longtime companion, Sally Wilbourn; and a large extended family. Worldwide news coverage of his passing attested to the mark he left upon the world. His final resting place is in Memorial Park Cemetery in Memphis.

BARBARA PITTMAN (1938–2005) moved from Memphis to Los Angeles, where she found work as a singer and bit-part player in the movies. She also sang on cruise ships for a time.

ELVIS PRESLEY (1935–1977), during his career, made thirty-three movies and won three Grammy awards, all for albums of gospel music. He was elected to membership in four music halls of fame: the Rock and Roll, Gospel, Rockabilly, and Blues. His home and burial site in Memphis, Graceland, is the pilgrimage site each year of more than 700,000 loyal fans from all points of the globe, and his estate continues to generate income placing him at or near the top of earnings from the estates of deceased entertainers.

REGINA REESE (1936–) left Sun and returned to Tupelo to finish her college education and become a high-school English teacher. She married, and she and her husband are now retired in Mississippi.

CHARLIE RICH (1932–1995), after his contract with Phillips International ended, recorded for several other labels, exploring an extensive repertoire of rock, jazz, soul, gospel, and country music. It was in the last field he attained his greatest success, being named the Country Music Association Male Vocalist of the Year (1973) and Entertainer of the Year (1974). He was one of Las Vegas's most popular entertainers for a time and is remembered also as a songwriter whose compositions have been recorded by a variety of artists. He and Margaret Ann, his wife, are buried side by side in Memphis.

BILLY RILEY (1933–2009) continued to perform right up until his death, a great deal of the time in Europe. After the 1970s he issued several blues-oriented CDs. He is in the Rockabilly Hall of Fame in Jackson, Tennessee. Bob Dylan has been quoted as saying Billy was his favorite rockabilly.

CECIL SCAIFE (1927–2009) moved to Nashville in the 1960s to be in charge of Sun's studio there and subsequently worked for major labels before founding the Gospel Music Association and engaging in successful music enterprises that allowed him to become a philanthropist. He helped found Belmont College's program in music-business education and established a scholarship there.

CHARLES UNDERWOOD headed for Hollywood when his tenure at Sun ended, continued writing songs, and found success as a record producer for musicians, including Herb Alpert.

J. M. VAN EATON (1938–) continued as a drummer, later songwriter and singer, after work with Sun became scarce. In the 1980s he became an investment banker in his hometown of Memphis.

SALLY WILBOURN (1937–) lives in Memphis and continues to assist the Phillips family in the management of their publishing, radio, and other holdings. She has maintained Sun Records and Sam Phillips memorabilia and has assisted researchers into Sam Phillips's life and career.

MARTIN WILLIS (1938–) retired from music and pursued a business career in Florida.

ACKNOWLEDGMENTS

I cannot adequately express my gratitude to, nor even here name, all those who have expressed interest in the subject of my Sun years. Hoping I have not omitted anyone, I would like to thank especially those who have read and offered comments on various drafts or chapters, including Frank de Caro, Jim Bennett, Lynn Mitchell, Rick Coleman, Bret Lott, Jack and Jeane Lavin, Will MacCalder, Russell Desmond, June Kost, Bennie Coates, Joanie Penniman, Leon LeJeune, Art and Donna Sterling, Anne Patin, Melvin Shortess, Elizabeth Burns, Michael Holland, Bruce Sharkey, John Stinson, and Mary Ann Sternberg. I also thank my student employees whose support through the years has afforded me time and energy to complete this project.

I have relied on the 1975 monograph *The Complete Sun Label Session Files (Revised)* for the chronology and personnel of studio sessions and acknowledge my great debt to the authors, Colin Escott and Martin Hawkins. *Billboard* magazine charts and reports were referred to in stating placement of recordings in national rankings and some historical background.

Thanks to John Singleton of Sun Entertainment Corporation for permission to use the majority of the graphics in this book, without which my narrative would have lacked a vital component. Added thanks as well to others, especially Robert Dye of Elvis Presley Enterprises, Inc., and Chelsie Lykens of the Roy Orbison Estate, who have shared visuals for use in the book.

I appreciate the efficient and tactful manner in which Margaret Lovecraft and the staff at LSU Press have initiated me into the world of book publishing.

I also must express admiration and gratitude to those pioneering students of early rock and of country music whose writings set the tone for the serious consideration of the musical genres Sun artists explored, including Peter Guralnick, Greil Marcus, and Bill Malone.

INDEX